Jesus, the Brother of James and Jude, and the Savior of the World

JANINE KREDELL

WestBow
PRESS
A DIVISION OF THOMAS NELSON

WestBow Press books may be ordered through booksellers or by contacting:

WestBow Press
A Division of Thomas Nelson
1663 Liberty Drive
Bloomington, IN 47403
www.westbowpress.com
1 (866) 928-1240

Cover art by Roberta Messner.

ISBN: 978-1-4908-0953-3 (sc)
ISBN: 978-1-4908-0954-0 (e)

Library of Congress Control Number: 2013917368

Printed in the United States of America.

WestBow Press rev. date: 11/12/2013

Thank you to Pastor Jack Shannon, Prescott American Lutheran Church; dear friends; Laura Markel, Charma Brian and Karen Harrison for your prayers and friendship. I thank God for the blessing of many Christian friends in my life. Thank you Roberta Messner, my talented artist and most of all, my husband David, the love of my life.

CHAPTER ONE

JESUS GOT THE MESSAGE FROM James and Jude. Come right now, your dear friend Lazarus is really sick.

Mary and Martha knew He had healed hundreds, maybe thousands of people in Judea and Galilee. At times they would ask Jesus with a chuckle if there was anyone who could be ill in Galilee; because He had healed so many people.

One morning Lazarus woke up and said to his sisters, "Find Jesus. I am very sick."

Martha said, "Really Lazarus? You feel that badly?"

Lazarus moaned, "Martha, please." Then he lost consciousness.

Martha screamed "Mary, Mary!"

Mary walked in and said, "Martha, what are you screaming about?"

Martha was sobbing," Mary, look at our brother. He said, 'I am sick, find Jesus,' and then he lost consciousness."

Mary said, "Oh no. Let me run into Jerusalem and find Mother Mary. She always knows where Jesus is."

Mary put on her sandals, ran and walked the five miles from Bethany to Jerusalem. Walking rapidly through the city, she saw Mother Mary outside her home.

Running now to the house, she shouted, "Mother Mary, Lazarus is very ill, and we need Jesus now. Where can we find him?"

Mother Mary sat down on the bench and pulled Mary down to sit with her.

Mary stood back up. "No, Mother Mary, this is serious. Lazarus is unconscious. We need Jesus now. Where is He?"

Mother Mary stood up and walked into the house, calling her sons James and Jude. "James? Jesus and the disciples are up in the Hazer area in Upper Galilee. Lazarus is very ill, and needs Jesus. Go with Jude immediately and bring Him back to Bethany."

Jude came over as he heard his Mother talking to his brother James. "We could take Hannah and Ezekiel and ride them up there."

His mother said, "No. It's too far for Hannah, she is too old, and Ezekiel has never been ridden. You will just have to run up as fast as possible."

James said to Jude, "Brother, grab your water and your sleeping bag and let's go."

Five minutes later, James and Jude were jogging out of the city, headed north. As they jogged, James and Jude talked. All their life Jesus had been their 'older brother,' the child, the teen-ager who never got in trouble. It was only three years ago, Jesus had stood up in their little Temple in Nazareth, read from the scroll of Isaiah 'The Spirit of the Lord is on me, because he has anointed me to proclaim good news to the poor. He has sent me to proclaim freedom for the prisoners and recovery of sight for the blind, to set the oppressed free.' Then He rolled up the scroll, gave it back to the attendant and sat down. The eyes of everyone in the synagogue were fastened on Him and said' I am He' and sat down (NIV).This was in response to the prophecy in Isaiah regarding the Messiah.

James brought up the subject of Jesus to Jude as they slowed to a fast walk on their way to find their brother, "Jude, would you have guessed we would be walking to find our brother Jesus to heal Lazarus?"

"James, would we even know Lazarus if it not for Jesus?"

"True, our little woodworking shop is a short distance from the home of Lazarus, Mary and Martha in Bethany. Jude, think of all the people we have met because of Jesus."

James, think of all the people we would have met if we had accepted Jesus as Savior when He changed water into wine at our family wedding?

Jude laughed," Right there is a good example of how God works in His time.

Mother comes up to Jesus and says, "We need wine."

Jesus said," It is not my time" and minutes later the entire family is drinking the best white wine of life. Our sister is happy, and our brother in law has no idea what happened!"

Remember how the people in Gergesenes told Jesus to leave when the pigs jumped off the cliff? They were Gentiles though and had no idea that the Savior of the World was walking on the earth!

James and Jude went into a fit of laughter at this because they too had not realized the Savior of the World was living at their house.

As they walked, they reminisced about growing up with Jesus Christ, the Savior of the World. As they talked they felt the fullness in their heart, knowing that their brother was their Lord. James and Jude decided when they delivered the message of the illness of Lazarus; they would tell Jesus of their belief that He was the Savior of the World.

They did find Jesus right where Mother Mary said He would be. James and Jude walked over and said hello to Jesus and the disciples. The disciples sat down and talked with each other about how their day was going, while they watched James and Jude walk with Jesus down the road.

Jesus said, "What is happening to make you walk all the way from Jerusalem?"

James replied, "Mother and Mary, the sister of Lazarus sent us. Lazarus asked for you and then lost consciousness. They want you to come to Bethany right away."

Jesus said, "Anything else?"

Jude smiled at James and said, "You see, He knows."

"Jesus, James and I had a long talk on our walk here. It was evident to all of us at the family wedding that you are the Messiah. We knew, but we just refused to worship you, as our Lord and Savior. We are very sorry for being your very stupid brothers."

James said," The Savior of the World has to be somebody's brother; might as well be ours."

Jesus laughed and said, "Well if the Son of Man has to have brothers, might as well be you two!"

James and Jude looked at each other with relief. Jude said, "Then will you forgive us for being stupid?"

"And not telling Mother and Father we knew you were at the temple in Jerusalem all the time they were looking for you?" James asked.

Jesus laughed. "Yes, of course I will forgive you, and I have taken care of you in more ways than one since you were born. My Father in Heaven knows all, and He told me that you would be talking to me today. My Father has plans for both of you, but I cannot speak of it today. I have people to see here in Upper Galilee, and then the disciples and then I will hurry to Bethany."

James said, "But Jesus, Mary was adamant that you come right away. Lazarus begged for you and then lost consciousness. I have never seen her so anxious."

"My Father in heaven knows all. He told me that the Glory and Power of the Messiah will be shown in Bethany. I need to see people here, and then I will hurry to Bethany. Why don't you go to the house of Lazarus and see if you can be of any help and assure them I am on my way?"

Jude said, "We can do that. If Martha is cooking, then we will gladly stay and help out. So shall we tell her you will be there soon?"

Jesus looked at James and Jude and said, "Tell them I am coming to Bethany and say nothing more."

Jude said to James, "Ok, then we are on our way to Bethany."

Before leaving, they knelt on the ground before Jesus, but Jesus said," James and Jude, you are forgiven. I love you and know you accept me as your Lord and Savior. As this time, don't talk about it except to family members who also know. Soon, you will understand these instructions."

James and Jude stood up, and Jesus gave them a hug before they walked away.

Jesus walked back to the disciples when Peter asked," What was that all about?"

"The brothers came to tell me that Lazarus was ill."

Peter said, "And the three of you had to go down the road to talk about that?"

"Well, there was some family business they wanted to talk about to with me. Anyway, Lazarus is sleeping, so we spend some time with the people here and hurry to Bethany."

Judas yelled in the direction of Jesus, "Those people want to kill you there! We should just stay here and continue what we are doing right now."

"No," Jesus said, "We need to go there. Besides Martha is probably cooking up something really good right now.

John laughed and said, "I doubt it. You made her leave the kitchen."

Jesus looked back and said, "We ended up compromising. I stood and talked to her in the kitchen while she was cooking. It worked out well for both of us."

Judas said," I love that family."

Jesus stopped and said, "Why? Because they fill up the purse every time we visit?"

Judas bowed his head down and said, "Ahhh, no. They are really true believers."

Jesus agreed, "Yes, I can agree with you Judas. Their faith in God the Father is strong, which is why we are going to visit them now."

The disciples had been with Jesus for three years and had seen him walk on water, calm the seas, feed thousands with five loaves of bread and two fish, heal the sick and raise children from the dead. They picked up their bedrolls and headed out. They walked, stopping to talk to people on the road. Jesus knew them all by name, remembering when and how He had met each one of them. If anyone they met had food, they shared it with Jesus and the disciples.

As they walked along the road, Jesus stopped, circling around to face the disciples said, "Martha and Mary's brother is sleeping, but I am going to wake him up. I want your support and prayers when I wake him."

Nathaniel yelled from the back of the group and said, "Jesus, if he is sleeping, he may not feel like having us come to visit."

Everyone nodded their head. A remedy as old as time; their mothers had put children to bed to sleep off a fever or stomachache.

However Jesus was talking about a different sleep: Jesus would always talk in simple stories with a deep meaning. This time the disciples didn't catch what Jesus was saying. They took him literally at his word. They didn't comprehend that Jesus would wake Lazarus from the dead.

Bluntly He said, "Lazarus died. We are going to Bethany and you will see the Power and Glory of My Father."

Then Thomas (also known as Didymus) said to the rest of the disciples, "Let us also go, that we may die with him."(NIV)

The brothers James and John were called the Sons of Thunder. They didn't make their special relationship with the Lord known to the others. With Peter, the three had seen the transfiguration and heard the voice of God. Today, walking together behind the other disciples, they talked about the strangeness of the day. Lazarus was dead, and whatever was Thomas talking about? What was Jesus talking about? They had seen Jesus bring children back from the dead, but a man who had been dead for what? Maybe four days?

If it had been four days, the entire mourning cycle would be in force. Lazarus was a wealthy, powerful man with many friends. There would be the hired mourners with their wailing flutes and the rich and powerful, and the everyday people who had had some contact with Lazarus. After three years of following Jesus, they knew to expect the unexpected. Every day was a new experience with the people of Galilee, with Jesus giving the grace of His Father: forgiving, teaching, healing and bringing all people closer to Him.

As James and John had surmised, Lazarus had already been in the tomb for four days. Bethany was a half hour walk from Jerusalem; a large crowd of friends, family and business associates had stopped their daily routine to support Mary and Martha with food and tears. Caiaphas the head priest from the Temple in Jerusalem was there with some Pharisees and Sadducees. It was exactly the circus James and John thought it would be, and then some.

Martha glanced out across the yard and saw Jesus and the apostles walking down the road. Martha picked up her skirts and ran down the road to meet Him, but Mary stayed in the house.

Martha walked up to Jesus, hugged him and said softly in his ear." I knew you could heal him, but I didn't know that you were in the far north of Galilee. Thank you for coming because I know you are the Son of God and a good friend of Lazarus."

Leaning back, Jesus looked at her and said, "Lazarus will live again."

"You taught us about eternal life and heaven the day I wouldn't come out of the kitchen. Oh, what wonderful things I learned that day."

Stepping toward Martha, Jesus held her hands in front of Him and said," Look at me. You know who I am. Believe in me and you shall never die."

"Jesus, I know you are my Lord, the Messiah, and the Son of God. I'll walk back and get Mary; then we will walk to the place where Lazarus is laid."

Walking back to his disciples where the disciples stood, Jesus chatted with his friends who had been with him for three years. Looking at all of them, he asked them to sit down on the grass with him. "Watch, listen and then believe what the Son of the Father can do."

Bartholomew turned and saw Mary and Martha, so he stood up. Jesus and the others stood up, and followed Mary and Martha down the road. Behind Jesus and the disciples, the house emptied out, and a crowd of people followed her, including Caiaphas and his entourage.

Walking over to Jesus, Mary fell at his feet crying. Seeing Mary cry made Jesus sad and he knelt down beside her. Jesus let the tears run down his face as well.

"Lord, I wish you had been closer to Bethany. If you had been in Jerusalem, I know Lazarus would still be alive."

The large crowd was all standing together in a hushed silence until someone was heard to say," Too bad he hadn't been there sooner. You know, one word from Jesus would have healed Lazarus."

"Mary, where is he now?"

"I will show you, Jesus. It is just off the road, not far away."

They walked up to the tomb, cut into rock with a large stone in front of the opening. Jesus looked at James and Jude and commanded them to move the stone.

Martha was horrified. She did not want to see her brother like this; dead, wrapped in strips, and with the awful smell of death. She looked at Jesus and opened her mouth to speak. "Lord?"

Jesus looked at Martha," You told me you believed. Let me show you again the Power and the Glory of God."

The brothers, James and Jude had moved the stone. Jesus lifted his arms and his face glowing, looked up to heaven.

The silent crowd could hear His every word and heard Him say in a clear and loud voice, "Lazarus, come out."

Everyone froze, looking at the opening in the rock. What would happen?

Seeing the same thing at the exact same time- a man wrapped in wide strips of cloth was coming out of the opening, one foot, then one arm. Pushing himself away from stone door, Lazarus, the sick man who had died four days ago- was walking out of the tomb!

CHAPTER TWO

THE DISCIPLES WENT TO THEIR knees; the crowd went right the ground and put their heads down. They wouldn't look up at first, but then many were screaming," Zombie! Ghost! Dead man walking."

Some of the people were stunned and silent; some were praying "Hallelujah!"

The disciples stood up while Lazarus got hung on the rock with the burial strips of cloth. Jesus had a big smile on his face and pointed to James and John, "Go over and help Lazarus; will you unwrap him so he can walk out of there."

Relieved laughter broke out from the disciples, watching James and John untangle the strips of cloth.

Mary and Martha had run over to Lazarus, saying to James and John, "Move it you two; let the sisters take over."

Peter had followed the sisters with his canteen of water for Lazarus; he had to be thirsty after what he had just been through.

Lazarus drank all the water, raised his arms high in the air and sang loudly, "Hallelujah," in the beloved melody for Sabbath worship at the temple.

Hearing Lazarus, the people stood up and responded to him. Singing the phrase loudly back to Lazarus; the disciples, the sisters, the Marys and Jesus lifted their arms heavenward.

Lazarus took two steps forward from the grave and sang, "And thou shalt love the Lord thy God with all thine heart, and with all thy soul, and with all thy might." (KJV)

Often the cantor at the worship service, Lazarus was chanting his part of the weekly service. The people standing had heard him sing at worship and knew the responses to the phrases that Lazarus sang.

Smiling and singing loudly with their heart filled with love for God the Father, the crowd sang the next phrase back to Lazarus, "Blessed is the man that trusts in the Lord, and whose hope the Lord is." (NIV)

Lazarus walked up and pointing to Jesus with both of his hands, turned and sang to the crowd," And thou shalt rejoice in every good thing which the Lord thy God hath given unto thee, "(KJV)

The crowd lifted their arms up and sang loudly," The Lord is my rock, and my fortress, and my deliverer" (KJV).

Lazarus wrapped his arms around Jesus and whispered something in his ear. Jesus smiled.

Scanning the crowd for his sisters, Lazarus turned and seeing them, he yelled, "Martha! Is there anything to eat in the house for me and my friends?"

Martha cupped her hands and yelled back, "We shall roast our best lambs! Everyone, please come back to the house for a celebration, for Jesus had brought Lazarus, my brother back to life!"

At the point, the crowd let out all their emotions; cheering, yelling, raising their arms in the air, dancing in circles, and releasing all the tension in their bodies.

Singing all together the hymns of joy, the crowd quickly moved back to the house for a feast instead of a wake.

The people seemed to know that Lazarus and Jesus would want some time together before greeting the guests. Still standing outside the tomb was Jesus and Lazarus. Some distance away were the disciples talking among themselves, but yet everyone was watching the two of them out of their eye.

Farther away were small groups of friends of Jesus, friends of Lazarus, friends of the disciples; talking, but still watching Jesus and Lazarus. The groups were responding to their reaction of seeing a man dead for four days and brought back to life and complete health. Did you see this? Did you hear that? Could you believe when he sang? Was that James and Jude who rolled away the stone? It was astonishing to all who had just witnessed the greatest miracles of their lifetime.

Watching Jesus and Lazarus walk down the road away from the house, Jesus stopped, turned and put both his hands on both of the shoulders of Lazarus. Reversing their direction, they walked back up the road, past their friends, and right into the house.

Standing back and people watching, Caiaphas, the High Priest and his friends, sick to their stomachs walked in the other direction, back to Jerusalem.

The friends of Mary, Martha and Lazarus all stayed because no one wanted to leave. Martha and all the Marys cooked up a feast for many people in a very short time. It was really quite odd how strangers kept stopping by the house with food, and then leaving with a smile. Martha said to her sister," More food?"

Mary replied with a smile, "Yes."

Martha asked again, "And we never ever saw that man before?"

Mary shook her head and said, "No."

Mother Mary was in the corner of the kitchen cutting up vegetables and she was smiling to herself. She had recognized at least one man, although it had been over 30 years since the last time she had seen him. The sun had gone down, and people were finally leaving to go home to their own beds.

The disciples and Jesus were all used to sleeping outside. One by one, they had grabbed their bedroll, and found a good place to fall asleep.

Peter, James and John went up to Lazarus when he was finally sitting all by himself.

Peter said, "What happened after you died, and where were you?"

Lazarus smiled and said, "Did you see Jesus put his arms on my shoulders? Well, when he did that, I no longer could remember. I just have a lingering feeling of love and light."

James looked at Peter and John. John said," We have an understanding then. We also have that same lingering feeling of love and light, from a time when Jesus took just the three of us up on a mountain. We know that it was something beautiful and powerful."

Lazarus said, "Do you remember what it is?"

Peter replied, "No, we can't remember either, but it is a good feeling."

Lazarus said, "I cannot tell you how much I love Jesus. I would shout to the world that He is my Messiah and Savior."

Peter said, "Oh, so would I, any and every time."

CHAPTER THREE

MANY OF THE JEWS WHO had come to visit Mary, and had seen what Jesus did, believed that He was the Savior of the World.

Caiaphas called a meeting of the Sanhedrin. "What are we accomplishing?"

Some of the men of the Sanhedrin asked. "Here is this man performing many signs. If we let him go on like this, everyone will believe in him, and then the Romans will come and take away both our temple and our nation."

Caiaphas, the high priest that year, spoke up, "You know nothing at all! You do not realize that it is better for you that one man die for the people than that the whole nation perish.' He did not say this on his own, but as high priest that year he prophesied that Jesus would die for the Jewish nation," (NIV)After seeing Jesus bring Lazarus back to life, many of the Jewish leaders planned ways to capture and kill Jesus, so the power would rest in their own hands.

The next morning Jesus took an opportunity to talk to James and Jude, His half-brothers. After performing His first miracle- turning water into wine at a family wedding, James and Jude had been cold toward Jesus. Walking down the road, arm in arm, laughing in the familiar way of close family; Jesus, James and Jude were recalling the memories of their youth A half mile away, still in sight, they could be seen sitting by the road; Jesus talking, James and Jude nodding.

Jesus was telling them that His Father had a special plan for James and Jude and would they promise to fulfill the duties and responsibilities that God would give them? James and Jude, their hearts filled with love for the Savior, said, "Yes, we will, with the help of God."

Jesus said to the brothers, "I say to you, whatever happens in the near future, you will see me again. Do you believe my words?"

Once again, James and Jude solemnly nodded their heads.

While Jesus and his brothers were down the road, Lazarus was back at the house talking to others. He was still answering the same question; where had he been the past four days? He gave all the same answer as he had to Peter, James and John. Lazarus had lingering feelings of love and light and that was all he could remember. Praising Jesus for bringing him back to life, he continued to call Jesus his Lord and Savior.

Jesus walked back to into the house and grabbed a piece of fruit. He said to Lazarus, "Did you get enough to eat last night?"

Lazarus laughed and said, "Did I? Yes, and so did 200 other people. We had several strangers dropping off all kinds of food last night, saying hello and then leaving."

Jesus said, "Really? How unusual is that?"

Then he heard a chuckle coming from the other side of the room. Jesus walked over and gave his Mother a hug. "How are you doing today, Mother?"

"Son that was a wonderful day yesterday. I hope more people left knowing you are the Savior of the World."

"Mother, that is up to my Father in Heaven, but it was a meaningful day to me as well. Mother, always remember I love you, and I thank my Father for choosing you to be my Mother."

Mary reached up and hugged her Son, tears in her eyes, she said, "Thank you, Jesus for saying that. You are my Lord and Savior. I thank God every day for His blessings."

Jesus looked at her and said, "Good. The day is coming, Mother, when I will leave, but I will return again. Remember that when all seems unknown."

Mary looked at her Son, with a question on her lips, but Jesus touched her cheek with His hand, "Just remember what I told you."

Martha glanced at Mary Magdalene and said "I know you are tired, but could I trouble you to ask Mother Mary's friends just to stay one hour and help up pick up the house?"

"Absolutely. You sit right down and your house will be clean before we leave."

The friends of Mother Mary left the house spotless while their dear exhausted friends, Mary, Martha and Lazarus took a nap.

CHAPTER FOUR

I T ONLY TOOK JESUS AND the disciples a half hour to walk to the Temple. House cleaning was on the mind of Jesus too. Before they reached the city gates, He stopped and said, "Men, gather around. I can tell you what we will find. The money changers are so plentiful now that they have been crowded out of their assigned area. I will not stand for it and their greed sickens me. This is the house of my Father, and we are going to clean it for Him. We will walk in there, move them right out of the inside of the Temple to the little area outside the Temple, where they are supposed to be. Now, they will not be happy about this, so we must be firm. Do you understand my meaning?"

As one, they answered, "Yes, Lord."

"OK, be ready to be physical. Don't hold back."

Andrew hesitated to say anything, but got his courage up anyway. "Lord, I am a bit older."

Jesus laughed, "Andrew, I promise you that the Father will give you all the strength you need to move those evil moneychangers. All of you might want to stop for just a moment, and see Andrew removing moneychangers from the Temple."

Clapping Andrew on the back, the men marched through the gate, straight for the Temple. They walked with such assurance and confidence, that people stepped back out of the way. Some people, who had no place to go, followed them.

Walking up the Temple steps, all could hear the money changers shouting out currency numbers for the foreigners in town. Exchanging their own currency for Jewish money, they would buy the unspotted lambs and doves for the Passover sacrifice to God.

Without a word, the disciples all each picked an area, and started picking up moneychangers, tables, chairs, and doves; without slipping on what the doves had left behind on the floor of the Temple; moved them out of the room, and outside the Temple.

Jesus headed toward the money changers, kicking the tables over, heaving the cages of doves, taking the money and throwing it in the air. Money changers not thrown out decided to run out, leaving behind their doves and money. Jesus had picked up a whip and was cracking it around his head. There were some scared moneychangers running out of the Temple, but the crowd loved it. They knew the moneychangers did not belong inside the temple and were happy to see them gone.

After the entire area had been cleared, Jesus stood in the middle of the room with the disciples, and the bystanders were leaning against the wall.

With a booming voice Jesus shouted, "My House will be called a house of prayer, but you are making it a den of robbers!"(NIV)

Everyone within a block could hear him. Many came running to either see what was going on. Jesus called to the bystanders to come and clean the Temple floor and throw the shards and pieces of wood that were once tables and chairs into the street.

Immediately almost one hundred people were cleaning; buckets of water for the filthy floor, sweeping splinters of wood and an hour later, the Temple was clean and spotless.

Forming a line to see Jesus, the blind and the lame were helped to move closer to the Lord Jesus who healed them all. Filled with joy, seeing so much happiness, it was inspiring, infectious and the many smiling, laughing children were running in circles. Singing and shouting, 'Hosanna to the Son of David,' in the now clean room, devoid of moneychangers, the Temple officials marched in.

It didn't take long for the Temple officials and teachers of the Law to come huffing up the stairs, mumbling and grumbling. Marching up to Jesus, do you know the children are shouting, "Hosanna to the Son of David?"

Jesus looked down at the little men, "Yes, and have you ever read 'From the lips of children and infants you, Lord, have called forth your praise'? (KJV)

'Hallelujah!' Jesus and the disciples sang as they marched right out of out of the temple.

Singing "And thou shalt love the Lord thy God with all thine heart, and with all thy soul," (KJV) and the people bowed down as the Word of God marched by.

CHAPTER FIVE

WALKING BACK TO BETHANY IN silence, each one was deep in thought about what had transpired that afternoon. Finally Jesus broke the silence and said, "How about that Andrew? How many men did he throw across the room"? Andrew answered, "Seven, Lord."

Laughing loudly with Andrew, the disciples had to stop. Now each one decided to tell about how good it felt to throw the crooks and their birds out of the sanctuary. When they started walking again, all were still laughing and talking as they entered Lazarus's house.

The brothers who were the sons of Zebedee were walking over to talk to Jesus. "Teacher," they said, "we want you to do for us whatever we ask." (NIV)

Our mother Salome, because she is your earthly relation, wants us to ask for a favor. We are pretty embarrassed to ask you, but Mother insisted. She knows that you are the Messiah, the Savior of the World.

Jesus folded his arms and said, "I know both of your parents have a very strong faith. I love them, just as I love you. What do you want me to do for you?" he asked.

They replied, "Let one of us sit at your right and the other at your left in your glory."

"You don't know what you are asking," Jesus said. "Can you drink the cup I drink or be baptized with the baptism I am baptized with?"

"We can," they answered.

Jesus said to them, "You will drink the cup I drink and be baptized with the baptism I am baptized with, but to sit at my right or left is not for me to grant. These places belong to those for whom they have been prepared." (NIV)

'When the ten heard about this, they became indignant with James and John. Jesus called them together and said, "You know that those who are regarded as rulers of the Gentiles lord it over them, and their high officials exercise authority over them. Not so with you. Instead, whoever wants to become great among you must be your servant, and whoever wants to be first must be slave of all. For even the Son of Man did not come to be served, but to serve, and to give his life as a ransom for many." (NIV)

Later on John had a chance to talk to his brother James. "That didn't go well did it?"

James replied, "Mother. We knew in our hearts what Jesus would say. We could have stayed with Father and fished day after day, but we chose Jesus and to follow all his teachings. Do you think we should say something to Him about how we should have known better than question Him?"

John looked at his brother. "Have you not noticed yet that Jesus knows everything, including our thoughts? He knew our thoughts then and he knows now. We just need to do what he told us to do; serving others. At least, that is what I am going to do, and not worry about how important I am to my parents or anyone else I know. I followed John the Baptist, and heard him say, 'There goes the Messiah.' From now on, that is who I listen to."

James and John were the first in the door of the house of Lazarus, Martha and Mary. "Lazarus, wake up!" yelled James and John.

Lazarus walked out into the room. "Funny, really funny; it works better when Jesus says it."

Jesus wasn't there to hear it though. He was in the kitchen yelling for Mary and Martha. "Do you have any food? I am so hungry."

Martha walked in. "I do, but you have to stand here and talk to me while I fix you something."

Jesus laughed. "Yes, I know that is our new agreement. Mary, come on in and sit down, you need to hear this too." So they laughed and exchanged stories of how each of their houses was cleaned that day.

After they ate and visited with the family, Jesus and the disciples left and went to the town of Ephraim, which wasn't an hour away from Bethany.

CHAPTER SIX

WHEN JAMES AND JUDE TOOK over the wood shop when their father Joseph passed away, there were times between jobs they would find Jesus and listen to Him talk to the crowds. Their Mother's friends, sister and sister-in-law would load up the donkeys, Hannah and Ezekiel, with food and clean and mended clothing. Traveling with their Mother and her friends to see and hear Jesus and the disciples, James and Jude would hear the Word; see the lame walk and the blind see.

Walking back from Bethany, James and Jude walked to their woodshop, located in the neighborhood where their Mother Mary lived. Grabbing their bedrolls and water, they decided to go to Ephraim.

"What I most regret James, is that we could not get past the fact that Jesus is indeed the Messiah. We could have enjoyed our time with Him more, if we had not been in such complete denial of the fact He is the Son of God."

"Even now, He still calls Himself the Son of Man."

"Jude, if he had not come down from heaven and our Mother was not His mother; He would not be the Son of Man."

"Maybe that is why we were so stubborn in believing that He was also the Son of God; we just knew Him as the Son of Man," James said, "I was so stubborn. I couldn't see it, didn't want to see it, and didn't want to believe it; I should have been a Pharisee."

Jude laughed at that. "Mother. Remember when she took us aside and told us the story of when the Angel Gabriel came to her?' Jude recalled. I was really stuck on the idea of an Angel talking to my Mother, telling her she would be the Mother of the Messiah. All the prophets in the past writings were reluctant to do what God had asked; but not Mother. She agrees to what God had had asked her to do right away and writes a song!"

"She is a special mother to us all." James said, "I was surprised at the stories she told us about Father. He had many visions from the Angel Gabriel: marry Mother; escape to Egypt, King Herod's dead, go back to your hometown of Nazareth."

"Just like Mother, he immediately obeys. He had to go to Bethlehem because he was a descendant of David."

"So is Mother." James retorted.

"So are you!"

"I'm going with the brother of the Savior of the World," James raised his arms.

Jude got serious." Don't think it is going to be all wonderful. Caiaphas would love to have Jesus dead. Jesus told us we have a special task from God. Jesus said He will be gone and then come back. I have a feeling that our love for our brother will have to withstand some extraordinary times in the future of our lives."

James sighed. "Yes, and with prayer and faith in our Savior and in God the Father, we will persevere in whatever tasks we are given."

Still reminiscing, Jude said, "What about the birth of John the Baptist? Mother walks over to live with Elizabeth and Zacharias, and Zacharias can't speak until John is born?' The Angel Gabriel appears to Zacharias in the Holy of Holies and speaks to him. It was just like He spoke to Father; your wife is going to have a child."

"Except," James said," Zacharias had been married to Elizabeth for years and years, and Father had just asked Mother to marry him."

"True, "Jude agreed. "John the Baptist would be the most important prophet, because he would tell the people about the Messiah."

"How did we miss that, Jude?" Everyone else in the family could see it. Father's brother Cleopas and his wife, Mary, our favorite uncle and aunt, saw it; and they live all the way in Emmaus. Salome, Mother's sister and her sons James and John knew it. Are we the most stubborn people in Galilee?

Nodding his head, Jude said, "Definitely top ten."

Raising his hands to the sky James said, "Well, Praise then to the Messiah, for his forgiveness of my stubbornness. Think of the miracles we have seen. Remember what message Jesus sent to John the Baptist? 'So he replied to the messengers, "Go back and report to John what you have seen and heard: The blind receive sight, the lame walk, those who have leprosy are cleansed, the deaf hear, the dead are raised, and the good news is proclaimed to the poor."

Jude laughed again, "Demons. I always think of Mary Magdalene when we see or hear a demon. Is she not the greatest witness for the power and glory of Jesus? Every time she tells the story of how Jesus healed her, I smile."

"Wait, James said. "Decide how close I am when I imitate Mary Magdalene the way she tells her story."

Raising his voice and his arms, he started. "There I was, just a mess. My hair was uncovered and always in tangles, walking around bare armed all the time. I wouldn't wear shoes, always barefoot, and the demons made me talk trash about Jesus everywhere I went. I made fun of Jesus, called Him silly names, and I looked stupid, acted stupid and talked stupid.

One day I was in Galilee, the demons had me mouthing off about Jesus, and Jesus had walked up behind me. I turned around, looked into his holy face and Jesus said, 'Satan, leave her now.' I just fell to the ground and then the most pure sense of peace came upon me. I bowed at the feet of Jesus and said, 'Thank you Lord', and He said to me, 'Stand up Mary."

I stood up. "Jesus said, it is okay with me for you to tell others you are no longer are possessed by a demon. You can tell people you have been healed."

I know many people in Galilee who still turn the other way when they see me coming. Now instead of talking trash, I would be speaking truth. I said, 'Lord, thank you for healing me and I will tell everyone the truth."

Standing with his arms crossed, Jude listened to his brother. "You got it down; the sound of her voice, the story, and her determination to spread the truth."

"Determination is right. That's why I can tell the story word for word, I have heard it so many times. However, "James continued, "She is so charismatic, so intense; you are compelled to listen and watch every time, if only to see the drama!"

"Determination and drama, we need more of that, James."

Nodding his head, James said, "Yes, and yes. We have let our brother down. Our cousins James and John, the Sons of Thunder, as Jesus calls them, stepped up and we walked away. We were stupid, and we need now to get smart."

Jude agreed, "I am glad we told Jesus in Northern Galilee we have finally come to believe that He is the Messiah. Whenever I see Joseph of Arimathea or Nicodemus, they warn me of the Sanhedrin talk; planning on killing Jesus as soon as the Passover is done. We need to warn Jesus."

CHAPTER SEVEN

JAMES AND JUDE KEPT WALKING until they found Jesus talking to the people about sheep and goats. He was explaining to them that God wants all people to love Him with all their heart, with all their soul and with all their might, and to love their neighbors as themselves.(NIV) This was a talk about loving their neighbors and not realizing that God above sees all and knows all.

"When the Son of Man comes in his glory, and all the angels with him, he will sit on his glorious throne. All the nations will be gathered before him, and he will separate the people one from another as a shepherd separates the sheep from the goats. He will put the sheep on his right and the goats on his left."

"Then the King will say to those on his right, 'Come, you who are blessed by my Father; take your inheritance, the kingdom prepared for you since the creation of the world. For I was hungry and you gave me something to eat, I was thirsty and you gave me something to drink, I was a stranger and you invited me in, I needed clothes and you clothed me, I was sick and you looked after me, I was in prison and you came to visit me.'

"Then the righteous will answer him, 'Lord, when did we see you hungry and feed you, or thirsty and give you something to drink? When did we see you a stranger and invite you in or needing clothes and clothe you? When did we see you sick or in prison and go to visit you?"

"The King will reply, 'Truly I tell you, whatever you did for one of the least of these brothers and sisters of mine, you did for me."

"Then he will say to those on his left, 'Depart from me, you who are cursed, into the eternal fire prepared for the devil and his angels. For I was hungry and you gave me nothing to eat, I was thirsty and you gave me nothing to drink, I was a stranger and you did not invite me in, I needed clothes and you did not clothe me, I was sick and in prison and you did not look after me."

"They also will answer, 'Lord, when did we see you hungry or thirsty or a stranger or needing clothes or sick or in prison, and did not help you?'

"He will reply, 'Truly I tell you, whatever you did not do for one of the least of these, you did not do for me.'

"Then they will go away to eternal punishment, but the righteous to eternal life." (NIV)

James and Jude looked at each other. Jude said, "That is difficult for me to understand."

James replied, "What he is saying is that we need to feed, clothe and help the needy and lonely. If it were Jesus on their doorstep, everyone in the crowd would do all the things he just asked for him. What Jesus is saying we are all children of God, we are all neighbors and we all need to help each other?"

Jude nodded his head." Yes, that would make a difference in the world. The crowd is so quiet; do you think they understand?"

James said, "Some do, some don't. Some will in the future."

James continued, "Religion that God our Father accepts as pure and faultless is this: to look after orphans and widows in their distress and to keep oneself from being polluted by the world." (NIV)

"Sitting out here," Jude said, "Reminds me of one of my most favorite days. Remember sitting by the lake, way up in Galilee and it was too far to walk home for dinner?"

James laughed," That was an awesome day. We had Mother Mary and all her friends, and nobody had any food except for that little boy with two fish and five loaves of bread, and Jesus turned it into a feast with food left over."

Jude said, "That was the best fish and bread ever. Just thinking about it; I never had fish or bread that good, ever!"

James laughed out loud. "That is a tough one. How about hearing from the disciples the story of Jesus walking on water, and Peter comes out to see Him.' It is hard to have that much faith in God you will walk on water."

Jude said," Wait, I got one for you. 'As long as I am in the world, I am the light of the world. When he had thus spoken, he spat on the ground, and made clay of the spittle, and he anointed the eyes of the blind man with the clay, and said to him, Go, wash in the pool of Siloam. He went his way therefore, and washed, and came seeing."(NIV)

James said, "That rocked the house."

Jude, "Yet we were the stupid brothers."

James replied, "Yes we were, and I plan to dedicate my life to changing my attitude, my life and words to reflect Jesus, who we know is the Savior of the World."

Jude nodded his head. "I agree. I make a vow to you, to God the Father and to the Savior of the World I will change my ways and follow Him always."

Jesus walked over to the disciples after he had given the benediction. James and Jude stood on the outside of the circle with other followers of Jesus, who came to listen as often as they could.

When Jesus had finished saying all these things, he looked intently into all their faces and said to his disciples, "As you know, the Passover festival is two days away—and the Son of Man will be handed over to be crucified."(NIV)

The disciples just could not understand this, but were afraid for an explanation. He has just declared what would happen. What was there to ask? First of all, why crucifixion? Only the Roman government had the authority for that to happen; Jesus and the disciples had had no contact with that government at all. Crucifixion meant death, and he had just raised Lazarus from the dead, so that didn't make sense either. Like students, no one wanted to be the one asking a dumb question.

But Jesus knew and He would go to the bank of Jericho where John the Baptist had preached. It was as He was retracing some of the steps of His life on earth, and staying away from the evil Pharisees until His time had arrived.

Now the time was at hand, and now the goodbyes would begin.

CHAPTER EIGHT

IRST WAS THE DINNER WITH Simon the Leper. Did Jesus heal him? He must have-who else could heal leprosy? Could Simon the Leper be the father of Lazarus, Martha and Mary? Possibly- why would he have a dinner and have all his friends and family present, including Jesus and the disciples? Simon the Leper, born and raised a Pharisee, saw the Son of Man raise his first born son from the dead. He had prepared a fabulous banquet for Jesus, but his daughter Mary is the one who made a lasting impression on Jesus and all who were at the banquet. Many of the guests had been living on handouts, sleeping outside every night, going without seeing their family, just to listen to Jesus talk about giving to the poor.

Now they were having a fabulous dinner in an opulent house, with people who openly called Jesus the Messiah, the Savior of the World, just days after Jesus declared He would die and rise again. The disciples were who had been on message for three years, were now getting mixed messages, and Mary, the sister of Lazarus, was about to show them the first of new messages.

Mary wanted to do something special for Jesus. What could she do for Jesus who brought her brother back from the dead? She did have some wonderful perfumed oil called Nard in a beautiful alabaster bottle her father had given it to her as a gift. The bottle of Nard cost as a much as younger men and any of the disciples made in wages in an entire year. People used it as a burial oil to overcome the smell of the dead. Lazarus had just risen from the dead and a new and a very large bottle had been given to her. Perhaps thinking that her father was getting older, but certainly not thinking that Christ would be crucified in a week.

A feast of the best delicacies with special ingredients prepared by Martha, were served to family and friends of Jesus. All were relaxing, talking about the weather and events of Jerusalem.

Jesus was also sitting and relaxing just outside the door, admiring the view and Creation. Mary walked out the door with her large alabaster bottle and asked Jesus if she could massage his feet. Jesus sat up and said, "Yes Mary, you may."

Mary broke the top of the jar, and poured the oil onto the feet of Jesus. She carefully massaged the perfumed oil on the feet of Jesus, wiping them with her long thick hair. The heavenly aroma brought everyone to their feet as they peered out the doorway. That act of love and respect for the Savior of the World was a humbling act and way for Mary to serve her Lord. Mary had found the way to thank Jesus and give him homage to her King for bringing Lazarus back to life.

Many of the people in the house understood the respect that Mary was showing Jesus. Her brother was alive and the only reason was Jesus. What is a year's wages for the return of a beloved brother?

The people in the house knew that Mary was a true believer; Jesus Christ was the Savior of the World, honoring Jesus as her Lord. Giving everything she owned serving Him as Her Master, giving Him the homage due to a King, wiping her hair across his feet- all of this showed Mary was a true servant to the Savior.

However, Judas Iscariot actually complained loudly as his priority was not the Messiah, but the money. Judas said he was concerned about the poor people and how that all that perfume just wasted on the feet of Jesus could have fed oh so many people. The truth? He was thinking how much of that money he could have stolen for himself. Jesus told Judas Iscariot right to his face- Leave Mary alone. The perfume was always for me, but for a later time.

He looked Judas right in the eye and said, "You will always have the poor among you, but you will not always have me."(NIV)

Judas turned and walked away.

CHAPTER NINE

IT WAS THE BEST PARTY. Everyone was so happy that Jesus had brought Lazarus back from the dead. Everyone there believed that Jesus was the Messiah. Everyone there brought something to sleep on and planned to get up early the next morning. After a big breakfast, friends and family started walking to Jerusalem for the Passover festivities, and to see the people who had traveled to Jerusalem.

Jesus, the disciples, Mother Mary and her good friends were the first to leave Bethany. Following behind them were Martha, Mary her sister, Lazarus and all their friends; headed for Jerusalem. Soon it was one extremely large group singing songs of praise; Lazarus was alive and Jesus was the reason why.

As they got closer to the city, they were surprised to see many people coming to greet them. Jesus told his two fastest disciples, the Sons of Thunder, to go and get a donkey. He even told them where to find a donkey and a colt and make sure to tell the caretaker, 'that Jesus has need of them and he will send them right away."(NIV)

It was Hannah and Ezekiel, the donkeys of Mother Mary, and John Mark was the caretaker. Ezekiel was a large white colt who had never been ridden. The friends of Mary had loaded him up several times for trips to north Galilee, but never ever had they attempted to ride him.

John Mark followed James and John running to Jesus with Hannah and the colt Ezekiel and whistled when he saw the enormous crowd around Jesus. The disciples took off their coats and laid them on the backs of Ezekiel and Hannah. Jesus walked up to Ezekiel, whispered in the donkey's ear, and scratched the donkey's head. John Mark cupped his hands for Jesus to get on the taller Ezekiel's back.

Ezekiel and Jesus walked through the gate into Jerusalem. The Sons of Thunder stepped in front of the donkeys and Jesus and loudly shouted. "Hosanna!"

The crowd roared back, "Hosanna!"

James and John yelled, "To the Son of David!"

The crowd picked it up, "Hosanna to the Son of David, Hosanna to the Son of David!"

Everyone in the crowd started spreading their coats on the road for Jesus, Ezekiel and Hannah to walk on. The disciples and other men started cutting off branches from palm trees and waving them back and forth in the air.

The disciples surrounded Jesus and continued to shout, "Blessed is He who comes in the name of the Lord!"

The crowd shouted back, "Hosanna in the highest!"

More palm branches were cut, and some were handed to the children who had run to the gate to see what was going on. All the children knew Jesus; they could always count on a blessings and a head rub whenever they saw Him. Running to the street, the children grabbed a cut palm branch and joined in the cheering.

Jesus and the crowd walked through the city of Jerusalem. The foreigners in town for the Passover asked, "Who is this?"

People in the crowd answered, "This is Jesus, the prophet from Nazareth in Galilee. He raised Lazarus after he had been dead for four days."

Mary Magdalene reached for Mother Mary and hugged her. A shiver went down the back of Mother Mary as she heard thousands of people and all the children cheer her son, Jesus, the Savior of the World.

People who could not walk and people who could not see came to Jesus that day at the temple and He healed them. In one day, the chief priests and the teachers of the law heard about the parade through the city, saw the healing, heard the children shouting, "Hosanna to the Son of David," and were just furious with Jesus. Loud, happy children, singing and dancing in a circle, only waving palms this time, always got on the nerves of the priests.

Jesus was too popular with the people. The people were questioning the temple chief priests about temple policies; policies different than what Jesus had taught to them. "Do you hear what these children are saying?" the priests asked Jesus.

"Yes," replied Jesus, 'Have you never read from the lips of children and infants you have ordained praise?' He turned around and walked down the steps of the temple and went back to Bethany where Lazarus lived and spent the night." (NIV)

CHAPTER TEN

THAT NIGHT THE CHIEF PRIESTS were talking about their anger, their loss of money, the throwing out of the moneychangers and what they would like to do to Jesus; Judas Iscariot came knocking on their door. Judas walked inside and said, "Would you like me to help you arrest Jesus while no one is around?"

The chief priests said, "Judas! We were just talking about that very problem. Let's call in the captain of the guard and he can tell what you can do for us. Then we will decide what we can do for you."

Judas told the priests Jesus and the disciples spent every night at the Mount of Olives, He would walk up to Jesus very late in the evening accompanied by the Temple guards and betray him with a kiss.

The chief priest said to him, "Judas, I think that plan will work just fine. We will send the entire guard and we will go too. I can't wait to bring that man into the Sanhedrin. How much money can I offer you?"

Judas still burning about the expensive perfume Mary put on the feet of Jesus said, "I think thirty pieces of silver would work."

The chief priests agreed, and the guard said, "We were thinking Thursday night."

Judas replied, "I can do Thursday night."

Killing Jesus was planned and paid at that time.

Of course Jesus knew all of this had transpired, so he stayed extra busy until Wednesday; going to the temple, preaching early in the morning until dusk. Mother Mary and her friends would walk up to the temple while Jesus stood teaching on the steps. They heard the Pharisees and the Sadducees try to trick him, or make him look stupid, but it always backfired on the church leaders. The crowd would either nod their heads at the answer Jesus gave, or just laugh right out loud at the Pharisees and Sadducees. At dusk, Jesus and the disciples would head for the Mount of Olives where it was cool and quiet. Mother Mary and her friends, the donkeys, Hannah and Ezekiel, would carry food and then go back to their homes. Again, Jesus would explain to the disciples this was not going to be a good week for any of them. He was going to die. He did not share this with anyone else, but the disciples. Mother Mary and her friends did not know when these events would happen. They had heard Jesus talk about leaving and coming back, but how this would happen, they did not know.

"Now there were some Greeks among those who went up to worship at the festival. They came to Philip, who was from Bethsaida in Galilee, with a request. "Sir," they said, "we would like to see Jesus." Philip went to tell Andrew; Andrew and Philip in turn told Jesus.

Jesus replied, "The hour has come for the Son of Man to be glorified. Very truly I tell you, unless a kernel of wheat falls to the ground and dies, it remains only a single seed. But if it dies, it produces many seeds. Anyone who loves their life will lose it, while anyone who hates their life in this world will keep it for eternal life. Whoever serves me must follow me; and where I am, my servant also will be. My Father will honor the one who serves me.

"Now my soul is troubled, and what shall I say? 'Father, save me from this hour'? No, it was for this very reason I came to this hour. Father, glorify your name!"

Then a voice came from heaven, "I have glorified it, and will glorify it again." The crowd that was there and heard it said it had thundered; others said an angel had spoken to him.

Jesus said, "This voice was for your benefit, not mine. Now is the time for judgment on this world; now the prince of this world will be driven out. And I, when I am lifted up from the earth, will draw all people to myself." He said this to show the kind of death he was going to die."

The crowd spoke up, "We have heard from the Law that the Messiah will remain forever, so how can you say, 'The Son of Man must be lifted up'? Who is this 'Son of Man'?"

"Then Jesus told them, "You are going to have the light just a little while longer. Walk while you have the light, before darkness overtakes you. Whoever walks in the dark does not know where they are going. Believe in the light while you have the light, so that you may become children of light." When he had finished speaking, Jesus left and hid himself from them." (KJV)

CHAPTER ELEVEN

WEDNESDAY MORNING, JESUS GOT UP before the disciples, but whispered to John, "I am going into town to see my family. You all have the power to preach and heal. Keep busy and I will be back tonight."

Immediately Jesus was in the woodshop of James and Jude, close to his mother's house.

He saw the brothers had put together a very nice table that week, but it needed some sanding, so he smoothed out the table and it was now ready to be oiled. Spotting some really nice pieces of wood, he thought he would make his mother a nice little sewing chair. While Jesus was measuring and cutting the wood, when his brother James walked in the door with a bowl of fruit.

James said, "Good morning Jesus. I knew it had to be you- always the early riser."

Jesus smiled and said," But I will sing of your strength, in the morning I will sing of your love; for you are my fortress, my refuge in times of trouble. I love that Psalm of David."

James walked up to Jesus and gave Him a hug and said, "Amen."

James said, "I just sent Jude over to get Mother. She wants to see you."

Jesus replied, "She is a mother. It's what mothers do, but I also wanted to see you."

James looked up from his fruit and said, "Why?"

Jesus sitting on a stool leaned forward with his hands on his lap. "James. I can read your heart. You know I am the Christ. I told you I would speak to you later when I saw you in northern Galilee. I need you to listen very closely and everything I say is true. When I am gone, people will look to a leader to bring all the believers together. The Father has designated you to be the leader. You are to organize the church in Jerusalem, delegate to others jobs that you do not have time to do, and to spread the story of my life, as the Son of Man and as the Messiah."

James bowed his head for a few seconds, looked up and said," Jesus, I will do as you ask, and I know your Father in Heaven will be there. I only need to pray to Him and He will answer me."

Jesus replied, "Yes James, which is exactly why the Father has chosen you. Love the Lord your God with all your heart and with all your soul and with your entire mind. This is the first and greatest commandment and the second is like it: 'Love your neighbor as yourself. (NIV) Remember this every day as all doors will be opened to you."

James said," I hate to ask this, but are we talking about the immediate future?"

"Yes James. I am going to die on the cross and be raised back to life on the third day. Do you remember the snakes in the book of Exodus, and God told Moses to put one on a cross and make the people gaze upon it to be healed?"

James nodded, "Yes, I remember that very well."

Jesus looked intently at James, "That was a foretaste and a prophecy of salvation. If the people gaze upon me on the cross and believe, they will be saved. Just as I raised Lazarus from the dead, I too will rise again on the third day."

James said, "This is the week?"

Jesus laughed and replied," Sorry to tell you, but yes, this is the week."

James said, "You are such a brother. However, you are my Lord and Savior; it shall to be as you said."

Jesus said, "I knew in your heart you would understand; not my Will, but my Father in Heaven's Will. This will be told to Mother in a different way, but she will know. Jude will be a much needed help to you. The disciples will want to scatter out into the rural regions in about fifty days. You will be needed to keep the sheep of Israel together during these times. I can promise that it will be exciting for you, but I am not looking forward to being on a cross holding up the sins of the world."

James said, "Oh Father God! Is this the only way?"

Jesus replied, "This has been planned since Eve ate the fruit from the tree of good and evil. Believing in me is the only way to salvation and heaven, and spreading the news that I rose from the dead on the third day is the work of all believers. Along with that, emphasize to the believers that each of them need to help each other out when the others are in need. Don't forget to talk about that. They need to act like believers, and not just think about themselves."

James said, "Wait, I hear Mother, Jude and the donkeys."

Jesus said, "Let me work in this chair for Mother. She needs something a little easier to get in and out of after sitting and sewing all day."

When Mother Mary walked in the door, Jesus held up the chair he had just put together for his Mother, "What do you think Mother? Come and try this chair out."

Mother Mary hugged Jesus and went over and sat down in the chair. "I like it, reminds me of that chair I liked so much at Elizabeth's house."

Jesus laughed out loud, "Oh those memories! Way back then with Cousin Elizabeth; Child soon to be born, son of God, born of a Virgin."

"Jesus, you are making me laugh! Jude came and got me, and I brought you some breakfast."

"Nice!" Jesus said. "This is good. Is it all mine or do I have to share with James?"

"You have to share with James! What kind of son did I bring up here?"

James laughed, "A perfect one, Mother. Jude and I want to confess to you while you are in a happy memory mood. We knew where Jesus was the entire time during Passover week. Remember? Jesus was twelve, gone for three days; Jude and I knew he was still at the Temple."

Mother Mary laughed and laughed. "Boys; no wonder I had gray hair at such a young age."

Jesus answered, "But a good heart, Mother- God, the Father knew you had a good heart. Mother, it is going to be a tough week-end for you, but you were the first believer that I am the Savior of the World. No matter what you see and hear, remember that."

Mary said, "Son, I believe in you. You are the Savior of the Word, and the brother of these two- James and Jude. I would stay and talk longer, but I promised Mary Magdalene we would go to the market before the Sabbath."

Turning, she asked Jude to take the donkeys back to her house. Jude said he would, but that he would just lead Ezekiel. She just laughed and said, "Well I guess you had better take the time to break him then," and she closed the door.

Jude turned and looked at his brothers. "Looks like I missed a great conversation."

Jesus said to James and Jude," Brothers, you need to know whatever Mary Magdalene says, it is the truth. You can believe her. When others scoff or disbelieve, you take her side, because our Father has given her the gift of speaking truth."

Jude said, "I feel like I have missed a half day, and I wasn't gone that long."

Jesus said, "No, its fine, but I did come here today for several reasons other than making Mother a chair. You are believers that I am the Savior of the World. This is going to be a long week, and your strength and belief in me will be needed by many people. This is the week ordained by my Father in heaven for me to die, go to hell and battle Lucifer, and then rise from hell and death and walk on this earth again on the third day."

Jude looked at James and said, "Oh. I guess I can postpone my plans this week. I thought I would be busy, but it sounds you will be busier. What is it we can do for you?"

"The first thing you will need to do is the first day of the week is get the word out that I am alive. The Pharisees will lie and spread money to cover up their crime. You must help Mary Magdalene and the women spread the word. You must stay resolute when the disciples tremble and run. The devil was given permission to sift the disciples and if you remember Job, Lucifer is a nasty supernatural power."

Jude replied, "Check."

Jesus looked at Jude," Then if that is covered, make sure the Upper Room is secured for a meeting at night of the first day of the week."

"Check and double check."

Jesus looked intently at Jude, "Do this all without ruining the surprise of the third day. Do not say a word about the surprise until the first day of the week. That will be difficult. You saw God the Father give me the power to raise Lazarus. God the Father will bring me back alive to the earth on the morning of the third day."

Jesus looked put his arms on Jude's shoulder's, "Did you ever hear the story about how Elizabeth's husband, Zacharias lost his ability to speak for nine months?"

Jude looked at James and said," I have reconsidered. I can do everything you have asked of me."

Jesus said to James," Now do you see why my Father in Heaven wants you to head up the church in Jerusalem?"

The brothers bantered back and forth all day, working on projects, and Jesus putting a finish on His mother's chair. His sister came by with lunch and her children. Jesus bounced the children on His knee and gave them His blessing, without saying anything to His sister about the upcoming week.

Finally it was time to get back to the disciples. He hugged his brothers and said, "Remember what I have told you. You will see me again. It won't be a fun week, but it will all be worth it. I am avenging Adam's sin, and soon if anyone believes in Me and is baptized, they will be saved."

With that he walked out the door and shortly he was back with his disciples. In the morning Jesus and the disciples walked back into Jerusalem.

CHAPTER TWELVE

BUT BEFORE THE EVENTS TO come, there would be one Last Supper together on Thursday. Jesus sent Peter and John to go and make the arrangements for the room and the food. Peter looked at John, and they asked Jesus, "Where do you want us to prepare for it?"

'Go and meet a man with a water jug on his head, and he will show you the room," Jesus said.

Peter and John went into the city, saw John Mark with the water jug and told him Jesus wanted to use the large upper room at his mother's house for the dinner. John Mark said," I will tell my mother. She will be honored that Jesus will be having the dinner there."

Peter replied, "It will just be Jesus and the twelve disciples."

John Mark said, "That is fine. I will have Mother purchase the food and leave it in the room for you."

Peter and John prepared the dinner for Jesus and the other disciples.

Jesus wanted to make an impact on the disciples, knowing that this was His last opportunity as the Son of Man. He washed their feet, but none understood that Jesus was modeling the behavior the disciples were to take.

After Jesus and the disciples had eaten the dinner, Jesus looked at them earnestly. "Listen to me carefully. I will not eat again until the Kingdom of God is fulfilled. I want you to do this to always remember me."

To emphasize the importance of the bread and wine, Jesus waited until after dinner was finished. Looking intently into their faces, he fed each disciple one by one, the bread and the wine.

Jesus took bread, gave thanks and broke it, and gave it to them, saying, "This is my body given for you; do this in remembrance of me."

In the same way, after the supper he took the cup, saying, "This cup is the new covenant in my blood, which is poured out for you."

"Simon, Simon, Satan has asked to sift all of you as wheat. But I have prayed for you, Simon that your faith may not fail. And when you have turned back, strengthen your brothers. "But he replied, "Lord, I am ready to go with you to prison and to death." Jesus answered, "I tell you, Peter, before the rooster crows today, you will deny three times that you know me." Then Jesus asked them, "When I sent you without purse, bag or sandals, did you lack anything? 'Nothing,' they answered." (NIV)

Jesus spent his last precious hour with his disciples sitting and reminiscing around the table. John looked across the table and saw Andrew and Bartholomew- covering their noses, turning their heads and coughing. John looked at Peter, and he seems to be choking.

John looked at Jesus, and he was motioning for Judas to leave. No one knew but Jesus, that Satan had entered the room. When Satan had entered the room, he had cursed all the disciples. Jesus then sent the traitor, Judas Iscariot, to meet with the soldiers all that Jesus had told them had been forgotten. The curse touched them all, except for the Apostle John. He alone, would be able to fight off Satan, until the third day at the tomb. John turned to look at Peter, and he was yawning.

"Oh Peter, don't yawn, then I will yawn."

"Sorry John, all of a sudden this fatigue hit me like a wall of bricks."

John yawning looked at Thomas, who was yawning. Everyone looked ridiculous, but Jesus who seemed oblivious to it all.

Jesus said, "Gentlemen, it time to leave."

They staggered out of the room into the fresh air, and it perked all the disciples up. No longer yawning, they left the house, singing hymns on their way to the Mount of Olives. Marching along together, raising their hands in the air, they were in the best of moods, putting their arms round the shoulders of Jesus; some would have thought maybe they had too much wine.

When they arrived at the Mount of Olives, Jesus asked Peter, James and John to go with him a little bit farther and pray with Him. On reaching the place, He said to them, "Pray that you will not fall into temptation." He withdrew about a stone's throw beyond them, knelt down and prayed, "Father, if you are willing, take this cup from me; yet not my will, but yours be done." An angel from heaven appeared to him and strengthened him. And being in anguish, he prayed more earnestly, and his sweat was like drops of blood falling to the ground." (NIV)

When he rose from prayer and went back to the disciples, he found them asleep, exhausted from sorrow. "Why are you sleeping?" he asked them. "Get up and pray so that you will not fall into temptation."

Being only a stone's throw- if the disciples had been awake, they would have seen the agony, the blood, the angel. However, cursed by Satan, they couldn't see the sins that Jesus bore for them and for us.

Jesus speaking to the disciples was interrupted by a crowd of thugs and armed guards from the temple, led by the most infamous man in the history of the world: Judas. As Judas approached Jesus to kiss him, Jesus asked him, "Judas, are you betraying the Son of Man with a kiss?" (NIV)

At that time, people began to act strangely. The guards knelt down before Jesus. Peter had brought a sword from the room and chopped off a guard's ear. Jesus picked up the ear and put it back on the man's face. The guards threatened to take everyone to jail; the disciplines ran. John Mark had been watching, and then running; losing his loincloth -running naked all the way home.

Peter followed at a distance, and saw that they had taken Jesus to the home of Caiaphas, which was near the Temple. John who was with him, talked to a guard he knew, and asked him to let Peter in, and John left.

A young girl came up to Peter standing in the courtyard of the High Priest and said I know you, "You were with Him."

Peter said, "No, I have never seen the man. I am just standing here getting warm."

Another girl came up and said." I have seen you with Jesus too."

Peter said," No, You are wrong. I don't know Him."

He didn't want to be arrested, but he just wanted to know what was happening to Jesus.

Then another man came over to the fire and said, "You talk like a Galilean, You must be a Galilean like Him, and you must know him."

Uncontrollably angry now, Peter screams." I do not know the man!"

Then Peter heard the rooster crow in the distance, and the words the Lord had spoken to him only hours earlier came to him, "Before the rooster crows today, you will disown me three times." (NIV) He looked up. Jesus was looking right at Peter. Peter had fulfilled the prophecy.

CHAPTER THIRTEEN

As FOR THE NAKED JOHN Mark, he had run into the house, into his room, grabbed a tunic and run to wake his mother up. John Mark told his mother all that had happened. John Mark and Mary hurried to Mother Mary's house.

Mother Mary asked John Mark, please run and ask my relatives and friends to come here right away. Within minutes all the Marys, Joanna, Susanna and Salome were there with Mother Mary, praying for the release of Jesus. Salome was the mother of the Sons of Thunder; she didn't know where they were. John Mark's mother, Mary and sister of Peter, didn't know where Peter could be. The sister in law -Mary, wife of Cleopas and brother of Joseph, was holding the hand of Mother Mary, offering prayers and comfort to her. Susanna's husband worked for Pontius Pilate, but Jesus wasn't there and Jesus wasn't at King Herod's. He was in the court yard of the High Priest; Caiaphas, the man whose number one wish was to see Christ crucified.

Mary Magdalene said," I can't sit here. Please allow me, Mother Mary, to find out what has happened to Jesus."

She offered to ride Ezekiel over to the temple area. All the friends agreed and said, go now! Please find out what has happened to Jesus.

John Mark was at Mother Mary's house, but he was not allowed to go anywhere near the temple. He cupped his hands for Mary Magdalene to climb up on Ezekiel's back and she galloped off to the temple.

He walked back into the house and said, "Did anyone know that Mary Magdalene can gallop on a donkey?"

Everyone laughed, and Susanna said, "No, but neither are we surprised."

Then they stopped laughing and continued to pray for Jesus and now for Mary Magdalene as well.

Mary Magdalene tied up Ezekiel in the alley of Caiaphas's house. She was dressed in black, and covered her head so she could get into the courtyard. Walking into the courtyard just as the sun was coming up; she was startled by a rooster crowing. Looking for the rooster, she turned around and saw Peter sobbing and shaking his fist as he walked slowly out of the courtyard.

She slid along the wall silently, but could only hear soldiers beating someone. Moving back against the wall towards the gate and walking as fast as she could, Mary Magdalene jumped on the back of Ezekiel and rode to Mother Mary's house. John Mark helped her off Ezekiel, but she was silent and did not answer his questions.

Mary Magdalene walked Ezekiel to Mother Mary's house. Her heart was heavy. She had so many questions. 'Why were they beating Jesus? Why had Judas kissed Jesus as John Mark had said? Where were all the disciples? Why was Peter sobbing and shaking his fist at a rooster?'

When she got back to Mother Mary's house, she told them what she had seen, and no one had any answers. Mother Mary said, "Let's pray once again, and then my friends, go home. We will meet tomorrow morning, but talk to everyone you can first and see what you can find out. Mary Magdalene, will you stay with me tonight?"

Mary Magdalene said, "Of course I will. Let me go take care of the donkeys. Friends, walk softly out there until we find out what is going on. Let's all meet at our spot tomorrow a little after dawn, which is soon approaching, and see what we can find out what has happened to Jesus."

Everyone hugged each other, and left.

Mother Mary said, "I am exhausted."

Mary Magdalene nodded and replied," I am too."

Mother Mary said goodnight and walked into her room. Mary Magdalene walked around her house, as she thought about what she had seen and heard that night and wondered what it all meant. Finding a cot, she lay down and fell asleep. The donkeys, Hannah and Ezekiel, had been standing at their listening spot by the window, and then they too walked into the barn and went to sleep.

CHAPTER FOURTEEN

PETER WASN'T SLEEPING EITHER. WALKING the streets of Jerusalem, not knowing where to go, he ended up at the shop of James and Jude. Early in the morning, they were both awake and going over the Word of God. They had memorized and studied the Torah just as their brother did. Mother Mary was as strict with James and Jude as she was with Jesus. It was quiet outside and James and Jude lived far away from the Mount of Olives.

Opening the door, Peter fell on the floor exhausted and sobbing. It was a warm spring night, and James urgently insisted Jude get water for Peter. James was not as large as Peter, but he easily rolled him over and pushed him up to a sitting position. Jude put the cup to Peter's mouth, but he only took a few gulps and then started to sob again.

James and Jude pulled off his robe, and poured water on his back. They wiped water on his face, and massaged his shoulders, still not knowing what had caused Peter to have a panic attack, a stroke, a nervous breakdown? What? Whatever was wrong with Peter? What could they do to calm him down? They drew long breaths with Peter; telling him to breathe in through his nose and out his mouth. Peter complied. Still as the tears ran down his face, it was more than five minutes before Peter could speak.

"I betrayed Jesus tonight."

Jude started to say something, but James gave him the older brother look - be quiet and listen.

"We were having the dinner at Mary's: the Upper Room. Jesus told us to look for a man with a jar of water on his head, and sure enough it was John Mark. John and I made the dinner, but everything about the night was so unusual. First he went around the table and washed everyone's feet. I was so amazed. The Messiah, The Son of God, is walking around the table, kneeling down before each disciple and washing our feet. Maybe it was like Mary perfuming his feet at the dinner at Simon the Leper's house;

Jesus wanted to do something really significant to show us His love for us, but I clearly did not understand what Jesus was doing for each of us."

He came to Simon Peter, who said to him, "Lord, are you going to wash my feet?"

Jesus replied, "You do not realize now what I am doing, but later you will understand."

"No," said Peter, "you shall never wash my feet."

Jesus answered, "Unless I wash you, you have no part with me."

"Then, Lord," Simon Peter replied, "not just my feet but my hands and my head as well!"(NIV)

"We were eating and Jesus had signified to John and me, that Judas would betray him. I looked at John, and he looks at me; I did not understand anything, as if I had lost our memory. Jesus looked at Judas and said something like, you can go now, and John and I have no idea what is going on.

That is the first stupid thing I do, but not the last. It only gets worse," Peter started weeping again.

This time James leaned in and hugged Simon. Simon pushed James away, "Wait; I have so much more to tell you."

"Jesus says to me, "Simon, Simon, Satan has asked to sift all of you as wheat. But I have prayed for you, Simon that your faith may not fail. And when you have turned back, strengthen your brothers."

"Lord, I am ready to go with you to prison and to death."

Jesus answered, "I tell you, Peter, before the rooster crows today, you will deny three times that you know me."

Then Jesus asked them, "When I sent you without purse, bag or sandals, did you lack anything?"

"Nothing," they answered.

He said to them, "But now if you have a purse, take it, and also a bag; and if you don't have a sword, sell your cloak and buy one. It is written: 'And he was numbered with the transgressors'; and I tell you that this must be fulfilled in me. Yes, what is written about me is reaching its fulfillment." (NIV)

Jude said to James, "He said, the devil has asked to sift all of you."

Jude looked at Peter and said," Peter, you are under the curse and spell of Lucifer, the angel who fell from heaven."

Peter just looked at Jude blankly, but James and Jude looked at each other with knowing eyes.

Peter began his story again. "Jesus had said to John that the man who dipped his bread in the cup would betray him. Once again, we don't get it. The eleven of us, without Judas, head out to the Mount of Olives like we do every night we are in Jerusalem and camp out there. We are singing our favorite hymns, we are singing in harmony, we are marching like school boys, and then Jesus says to the other eight, you can camp here, and Peter, James and John follow me for prayer. He tells us to sit under this tree and pray that we don't fall into temptation, and he walks about 100 feet away."

"All of a sudden, I couldn't keep my eyes open, let alone pray. Jesus comes back and says "why are you sleeping? I need you to pray that you do not fall into temptation."

While he is standing right in front of us, we say sure,' we can do that'. We are wide awake while Jesus is talking to us, and standing in front of us and as soon as he walks away, the three of us pass out again."

At least Peter is not crying right now, but James and Jude are physically supporting him and listening to his every word as Peter is remembering the night.

Peter continued, "We heard soldiers- we walked over to see what is going on, and see Judas leading one hundred soldiers. It was living in a nightmare. John and I just looked at each other. Suddenly, we are not tired. Judas comes up and gives Jesus a kiss on the cheek. Judas never ever kissed Jesus on the cheek. I don't let him wash our feet; I fall asleep during prayer. Then again I do something crazy thing. While we were in the Upper Room, my sister Mary had a couple of swords crisscrossed on the wall as decoration. Jesus is saying even though we have gone everywhere with nothing on our backs and no food, now we are going to need swords. Bring a sword to the Mount of Olives. Fine, Jesus wants a sword; I grab a sword."

"However, when I see those soldiers grab Jesus, I get absolutely uncontrollably angry, and I take that sword and I slash downward with it, and cut off the soldier's ear. "Peter looks down. Slowly he says, "I slashed downward and cut off that poor man's ear. After all the listening to Jesus for three years, blessed are the peacemakers and I cut off an ear." Peter sighed and the tears flowed down his face.

"Of course, Jesus picked the ear up, and put to his head, and healed him, and walked off with the soldiers. The soldiers yelled at us, we had better run, if they caught us they would arrest us for treason."

"So I ran- right past John Mark who had lost his underwear, I don't know what that young man was doing out that night. His mother will have his hide." Peter smiled for the first time.

"Now, the worst part: I am running with John, and he knows Nicodemus and Joseph of Arimathea, and when he was working with John the Baptist, he baptized many a Pharisee; he knows someone at the gate of Caiaphas's house and gets us in."

Peter is sobbing uncontrollably again. Jude goes and gets a bottle of wine. James is massaging his shoulders and Peter's fever has left him, but Peter is still in emotional and physical distress.

Peter says, "I am going to say it quickly and I hope never to say it again. A young girl comes up and says I know you, you were with him. I say no, I have never seen the man. I am just getting warm. Another girl comes up and says I have seen you with Jesus too. I say, No, You are wrong. I don't know him. The sun is starting to rise and I hear a rooster, but I don't think anything of it, I am trying not to be arrested. Then a man comes over to the fire and says, you talk like a Galilean, You are a Galilean, and you know him. So I get huffy and I yell out, I do not know the man! I hear the rooster, I look up. There is Jesus looking at me. I had just fulfilled the prophecy."

Peter curled up in a fetal position, and just sobbed and sobbed.

James and Jude put their hands on Peter, and began to pray to God the Father.

James prayed, "And the prayer offered in faith will make the sick person well; the Lord will raise them up. If they have sinned, they will be forgiven. Therefore confess your sins to each other and pray for each other so that you may be healed." (NIV)

Jude prayed. "To those who have been called, who are loved in God the Father and kept for Jesus Christ: Mercy, peace and love be yours in abundance. But you, dear friends, by building yourselves up in your most holy faith and praying in the Holy Spirit, keep yourselves in God's love as you wait for the mercy of our Lord Jesus Christ to bring you to eternal life." (NIV)

James and Jude kept praying for Peter until he finally did fall asleep. However, it was a fitful sleep and he called out many times, Jesus. Jesus.

Chapter Fifteen

THE ONLY ONE NOT SLEEPING was Jesus. He was being slapped, spit on and questioned by the high priest.

Jesus said, "You have heard me speak. If I have said something wrong, tell me. If not, why are you hitting me?"

The high priest asked Jesus, "Tell us if you are the Christ, the son of the Living God."

Jesus replied, "Yes, it is as you say."

The high priest tore his clothes and said, "It is blasphemy! "(NIV)

And for this sentence of truth, the Sanhedrin, the council of the temple, decided to put Jesus, the Savior of the World, to death. The man they had all just see put an ear back on a man's head that night, raise Lazarus from the dead, and in their own temple see Jesus heal the blind, the deaf, the lame; decided that such a healer and teacher of all people must die before the Sabbath.

Jesus looked at them and said, "And you will see the Son of Man sitting on the right hand of God and coming on the clouds."

The old men of the Sanhedrin just started screaming, "You will die!" They spit on him, and hit him with their fists. (NIV)

The Pharisees and the Sadducees could yell all they wanted, 'you will die,' but even the donkeys, Hannah and Ezekiel, knew that a religious temple council cannot actually execute a man. Only the Roman governor had the power to put a criminal to death and his name was Pontius Pilate.

Caiaphas and the Sanhedrin, the religious leaders of the Jews, would take Jesus to Pontius Pilate. They must tell a Roman that a Jew must die because he said he is the Christ. A person saying, I am the Christ, is not a crime worthy of death- yet the death of Jesus was the only punishment the Sanhedrin would accept.

Judas was also headed to the temple with his 30 pieces of silver. Apparently he had heard that his little kiss was going to cost Jesus, his friend of three years, his life, and all of a sudden, the silver just didn't seem that important. He told the chief priest he had made a mistake and Caiaphas stood up and laughed at Judas.

Judas threw the silver on the floor of temple, went out the door, out of the city, and took his own life. It was a gruesome death and fitting for the man who betrayed the Savior. Hearing Judas was dead; the priests picked up the 30 pieces of silver, bought land and buried the body of Judas there. It was called the Potter's Field, where the unknown are buried; and another prophecy spoken was fulfilled.

Mother Mary and friends got to the temple just as the guards were taking Jesus to the palace of Pontius Pilate. As women, they had to stand in the back of the crowd, but there they could observe everyone. They heard Pontius Pilate ask Jesus," Are you king of the Jews?"

Jesus replied," Yes, it is as you say." Pontius Pilate listened as the chief priests went on and on and on with accusations. Jesus didn't look and He didn't answer. Pontius Pilate had never seen this. Calmly Jesus stood- this man accused of a crime, facing the death penalty, behaving as if He was the King; superior to all accusers.

Pontius Pilate heard that Jesus was from the province of Galilee. Therefore, Jesus must go to the King of Galilee, Herod. The one who beheaded and killed John the Baptist could take this problem off of Pilate's hands. If Herod thought Jesus might do a miracle, talk to him, he was mistaken. Herod saw he was wasting his time, so he sarcastically ordered a kingly purple robe and a crown of thorns (which symbolizes sin) be put on him, and sent him back to Pontius Pilate.

The wife of Pontius Pilate told her husband that she had had a terrifying dream about Jesus and the frightening consequences if Pilate put him to death. He listened to her, and he listened to Herod. But in the end, Pontius Pilate listened and gave in to the chief priests. He gave the command for the crucifixion to be carried out that very day.

Waiting for the chief priest, waiting for Pontius Pilate, waiting for King Herod then again waiting for Pontius Pilate, the guards decided to spend their waiting time amusing themselves by whipping Jesus with leather straps, spitting, blindfolding, and still waiting -whipping Jesus again. Even with the loss of blood and tremendous pain, Jesus did not speak, nor did he have anything to drink.

Joanna's husband worked in the household of Pontius Pilate. He told Joanna, that the wife of Pontius Pilate had tried so very hard to stop the crucifixion. Mother Mary and her friends were speechless and terrified of the mob of screaming people yelling, 'crucify him'. They had never ever seen any of these people. Where had they come from? The women stood at the far back against the wall, just stunned. How could this be happening? Didn't they just have a parade with Jesus and a tremendous crowd of people shouting Hosanna? Where were those people now?

When the governor Pontius Pilate had given the order for crucifixion, what could they do? The guards were already putting the cross together and strapping it on the back of Jesus. There weren't any disciples around. They knew that Jesus had the power to just walk away, but why wasn't he?

CHAPTER SIXTEEN

THE WOMEN DID NOT REALIZE that the prophecies and promises from God were about to come true. Jesus Christ was the son of God, who had to die and rise again for our sin; it had been planned for our salvation, our only way to eternal life.

However, no one at that time was thinking of that. They were looking at a bent over man, covered with blood and too exhausted to carry his own cross.

Simon from Cyrene was taken out of the crowd by the Roman soldiers. Told to carry the cross for Jesus, he was just a visitor in town for the Passover Week with his two young sons. Mother Mary, friends and believers of Jesus were all following Simon of Cyrene and sobbing. They followed the soldiers, the man with the cross, the two thieves who were going to die, and the Lord to Golgotha, a hill outside of the city.

Peter, James and Jude could see from the wood shop what was going on, and were completely helpless. James said, "We need to pray to God. Think of what Jesus has told us. He told us he would die for us. He told us that several times, yet He also told us to believe in Him. Let us pray that God will give understanding."

Peter with his face still wet with tears said," I am going to pray for God's forgiveness."

Jude said," I am saying, there is more to come. This is not the end."

Peter said, "You just saw the cross and Jesus."

Jude looked at Peter and said slowly." This is not the end. There is more. I am going to change my clothes and cover my head, and go to Golgotha to see what is now happening."

Peter began to weep again. "I can't."

James looked at Jude and said," I am going to stay with Peter. We will fast and pray unceasingly. Look for Mother too, and make sure she has support through this."

Jude said, 'Ok,' and five minutes later slipped out the door and found a place where he could see the Savior of the World nailed to the cross, and then lifted up for the people to see.

The women stood back behind the crowd as the procedure and method of killing Jesus continued. The Pharisees and leaders of the temple made fun of him, yet he didn't come down off the cross. Jesus ignored the people who attempted to humiliate him.

Instead He asked His Father in heaven to forgive his murderers. He promised the thief next to him that he would be in heaven with him that very day, and he told his mother that John, the only apostle there at Golgotha, would take care of her for the rest of her life.

Mary Magdalene stepped aside with Joanna, Salome, the sister of Mary, Susanna and Mary, the sister of Lazarus, for a moment. She said," You know Mother Mary will not be able to take care of the body. She wants me to stay with her right now, so do you think any of you can go and buy burial spices right now?"

Salome answered, "You know us, Mary Magdalene and we will do anything for our Lord."

Joanna said, "The Sabbath is getting close, we need to get them, but we won't be able to use them until the day after the Sabbath."

Salome said, "We will get the spices, I will keep them at my house, and then at dawn after the Sabbath we will go to the tomb with the spices."

Susanna said, "Does anyone know where our Lord is to be buried?"

Mary Magdalene said, "Joseph of Arimathea already went to Pilate and is going to donate his burial place, but I will find out where it is and let you know."

Mary said, "You will be here then with Mother Mary."

Mary Magdalene said, "I will be with her. You can find me here, or I will see you at dawn after the Sabbath."

They all hugged and started crying, and then rushed away. They had to get the spices before the Sabbath.

The friends of Mother Mary, who had taken care of Jesus and the disciples during his ministry, pooled all their money, took the spices to Salome's house, and hurried back to Golgotha. It was near the end of the life of Jesus, the son of man. The sun had already disappeared at noon for three hours and it was completely dark. People came running up the hill saying the curtain protecting the Holy of Holies had been ripped from top to bottom.

People in the ages to come would say the ripping of the curtain in half signified that Jesus Christ had now become the way to God the Father, and no longer the high priest at the temple.

Jesus cried out. "Why has my Father forsaken me?" and then his final words "Into your hands I commend my spirit, "and he died. (NIV)

CHAPTER SEVENTEEN

W HY AT THIS EXACT MOMENT?
This was the exact moment when the lambs were being slaughtered for the Passover dinner. The earth shook in a terrible earthquake. The sun had been dark for hours. People who had been dead for years got out of their graves and walked into the city. The Roman centurion in charge said," Surely this was a righteous man."

John the apostle, Mother Mary, Mary Magdalene and Salome watched the Roman soldier break the legs of the others on the crosses, and pierced the side of Jesus, knowing he was dead. The blood and water of Jesus gushed out of his body, which is impossible to happen to people after they have died. This fulfilled the prophecy of the Old Testament, "Not one of his bones will be broken," and "they will look on the one they have pierced."

From a distance they also watched two members of the Sanhedrin, Joseph of Arimathea and Nicodemus, secret followers of Jesus Christ, take down his body. They took it to the nearby tomb owned by Joseph-recently cut in the stone. He had seventy–five pounds of spices with him, wrapped the body of Jesus in strips of linen, then in myrrh and aloes, and with the help of other men, rolled the massive stone in front of the tomb.

John, Mother Mary and Mary Magdalene walked back into Jerusalem slowly without saying a word, with tears silently running down their cheeks. John had a house close to Mother Mary and said, "Come over tonight.

Mother Mary started to shake her head no, but Mary Magdalene said, "Go ahead, Mother Mary. It is what your son wanted you to do. I will take care of the donkeys and see you tomorrow."

The tears started running down Mother Mary's face, and John reached for her hand, and they walked the short distance to his house. Mary Magdalene went and fed the donkeys, not knowing that John Mark had already fed them. Being a young colt, it seemed Ezekiel had a bottomless stomach and he was perfectly fine with some extra oats. Mother Mary was having the same feelings; only she felt it was a bottomless heart. She had said to the apostle John, "How can this all be happening? Did you see any of the disciples at all today?"

John had said, "Peter is at the shop of James and Jude. He is staying there. James and Jude took turns coming to the bottom of the hill. The rest of them I could see them in the far distance. Judas threw his 30 pieces of silver at Caiaphas and Judas left and hung himself. The Pharisees decided to buy the land where Judas died and make a Potter's Field out of it."

Now John looked and said to Mother Mary, "Jesus told us many things. Remember when he raised Lazarus after his fourth day in the tomb? Jesus said many times to the disciples that the Son of Man must die, but there always seemed like he wanted to say more. You are exhausted and so am I. I don't know if you can sleep, but you should go and lie down anyway."

"John, you are right. I need to pray and I need some time to myself. We can walk to temple together tomorrow."

John and Mary didn't sleep much, but kept going over their memories of the person who meant the most to them in their life. The next day John said, "Mother Mary, I don't want to go to the temple and hear a priest preach his false righteousness today. I think we should sit down with Mary Magdalene and share our memories of Jesus. Maybe we can gain some understanding into this week."

Just then Mary Magdalene knocked on the door and announced, "For the first time, I don't feel like going to temple. It is just going to be a finger pointing contest."

John said, "We all agree. Let's have breakfast, and share our best memories of Jesus."

The tears started running down Mother Mary's face, and John reached for her hand.

Mary Magdalene went and fed the donkeys, not knowing that John Mark had already fed them. Ezekiel thought, hey, this must be a feast day! Hannah listened to John and Mother Mary and her heart was sad. How could this all have happened this week? She remembered the stories that her mother Sarah had told her of Jesus' birth. Hannah lay down and wondered what would happen to them now.

Mother Mary started to shake her head no to memories, but Mary Magdalene said, "Go ahead Mother Mary. I will go with you to the grave tomorrow. It is best if you talk, and we will listen. It is what Jesus wanted you to do."

"I have things to tell you I haven't talked about since my husband Joseph died. First of all, you need to know that Joseph is not the father of Jesus."

Mary Magdalene and John turned around slowly and looked at Mother Mary.

Mary Magdalene said," I don't know about you John, but breakfast can wait right now. How about we all sit down?"

Mother Mary said, "I was asked by Jesus not to tell these stories but I have always kept them close to my heart. God the Father has blessed me in ways I still don't understand, I know it will feel good for me to finally tell you about the miraculous birth of Jesus."

Beginning her story, sitting in the chair her son had made for her that week, she looked at her nephew and said, "John, remember when you followed John the Baptist? His mother Elizabeth was my cousin. Zechariah and Elizabeth were very old and did not have children. Zechariah's name was drawn in a lottery to go to the temple and work one of the feast days. He was so old; he never expected that he would be chosen to work in the Temple and enter the Holy of Holies. He was so excited about going. He was even more excited when he returned home."

"However, he had to write to Elizabeth just what had happened during his time serving in the temple. "Then an angel of the Lord appeared to him, standing at the right side of the altar of incense. When Zechariah saw him, he was startled and was gripped with fear. But the angel said to him: "Do not be afraid, Zechariah; your prayer has been heard. Your wife Elizabeth will bear you a son, and you are to call him John. He will be a joy and delight to you, and many will rejoice because of his birth, for he will be great in the sight of the Lord. He is never to take wine or other fermented drink, and he will be filled with the Holy Spirit even before he is born. He will bring back many of the people of Israel to the Lord their God. And he will go on before the Lord, in the spirit and power of Elijah, to turn the hearts of the parents to their children and the disobedient to the wisdom of the righteous—to make ready a people prepared for the Lord."

"Zechariah asked the angel, "How can I be sure of this? I am an old man and my wife is well along in years."

The angel said to him, "I am Gabriel. I stand in the presence of God, and I have been sent to speak to you and to tell you this good news. And now you will be silent and not able to speak until the day this happens, because you did not believe my words, which will come true at their appointed time."

Meanwhile, the people were waiting for Zechariah and wondering why he stayed so long in the temple. When he came out, he could not speak to them. They realized he had seen a vision in the temple, for he kept making signs to them but remained unable to speak." (NIV)

"Even though it was the angel Gabriel telling him this, Zechariah didn't believe him, so the Angel took his voice away until John was born."

John and Mary Magdalene looked at each other in amazement. They had never heard any of this. Mother Mary said, "Oh there is more. The Angel Gabriel came to me and said that I would become pregnant with the Savior of the World. I lived in Nazareth. I was a very young girl and a virgin, but had fallen in love with Joseph who was older than me, and a descendant of David."

"Gabriel appeared to me and said, "Greetings, you who are highly favored! The Lord is with you."

"Mary was greatly troubled at his words and wondered what kind of greeting this might be. But the angel said to her, "Do not be afraid, Mary; you have found favor with God. You will conceive and give birth to a son, and you are to call him Jesus. He will be great and will be called the Son of the Most High. The Lord God will give him the throne of his father David, and he will reign over Jacob's descendants forever; his kingdom will never end."

"How will this be," Mary asked the angel, "since I am a virgin?"

The angel answered, "The Holy Spirit will come on you, and the power of the Most High will overshadow you. So the holy one to be born will be called the Son of God. Even Elizabeth your relative is going to have a child in her old age, and she who was said to be unable to conceive is in her sixth month. For no word from God will ever fail."

"I am the Lord's servant," Mary answered. "May your word to me be fulfilled." Then the angel left her. (NIV)

John and Mary Magdalene are leaning forward with their faces leaning on the palms of their hands. Mary Magdalene said, "Well, what did Joseph say about all of this? Why didn't he just walk away?"

Mother Mary smiled and said, "Gabriel also appeared to Joseph."

"Because Joseph her husband was faithful to the law, and yet did not want to expose her to public disgrace, he had in mind to divorce her quietly. But after he had considered this, an angel of the Lord appeared to him in a dream and said, "Joseph son of David, do not be afraid to take Mary home as your wife, because what is conceived in her is from the Holy Spirit. She will give birth to a son, and you are to give him the name Jesus] because he will save his people from their sins." (NIV)

"Gabriel then told me about Elizabeth, and that she was six months pregnant with John, and suggested I go and visit Elizabeth, and I said, 'I am the Lord's servant and it shall be as you said.' The next morning I headed out, and it was a good thing. Elizabeth knows all the prophecies, and as soon as she saw me, I could see John moving inside of Elizabeth. It was an amazing time, and I stayed three months and when I came back to Nazareth I was pregnant with the Savior of the World."

The tears started running down Mother Mary's face. "I have to remember what Gabriel said,' For nothing is impossible with God.' I rode home on the donkey Zechariah and Elizabeth gave me. Do you remember that crazy beast Sarah? She was my donkey, and we did some traveling together that is for sure. I sang all the way home, my soul praises the Lord and my spirit rejoices in God my Savior. From now on generations will call me blessed. I just don't feel very blessed right at this moment," and tears ran down her face again.

Mary Magdalene said, "Do you want to rest for a little while, Mother Mary?"

"No", she dried her eyes and with a small smile said, "There is a lot more you need to hear. How about you? Are you up to this?"

John and Mary Magdalene nodded their heads.

"So I went home to my house, Joseph and I delayed our engagement, decided not to tell anyone that I was pregnant, or that the angel Gabriel had appeared to us. I was young and in good physical condition and I took good care of myself. However, we didn't know how we would handle the talk when Jesus was born." She used her towel to wipe her eyes again.

"Then the perfect solution came along," Mother Mary said. "Caesar Augustus, sitting on his throne in Rome, said we were all to travel to the towns of our great grandfathers. Well, for us, that was Bethlehem. Perfect. Joseph finished up his projects, collected his pay, packed a few of his most necessary tools, picked me up, put me on Sarah and we were on our way to Bethlehem. We got to Bethlehem just in time. I am in labor but there was not one place to go, no time to find a cousin because I was in labor. We took Sarah the donkey into the stable; I sat down on the straw pile. Five minutes later, I told Joseph, "The baby is coming right now, so you better be ready to help out."

Mary Magdalene said, "That quick? Where did you put baby Jesus?"

Mother Mary said, "I wrapped him in swaddling clothes, and the only place that we could put him was the manger. I wasn't worried. God had taken care of me for nine months, and the delivery of baby Jesus was easy. He was healthy, Joseph was relieved we had made into town, and everything was just fine. I am resting with Jesus, and walking into the stable are seven shepherds. They are all really excited, talking very fast but really quietly as they keep peeking at Jesus!"

"An angel of the Lord appeared to them, and the glory of the Lord shone around them, and they were terrified. But the angel said to them, "Do not be afraid. I bring you good news that will cause great joy for all the people. Today in the town of David a Savior has been born to you; he is the Messiah, the Lord. This will be a sign to you: You will find a baby wrapped in cloths and lying in a manger." Suddenly a great company of the heavenly host appeared with the angel, praising God and saying, "Glory to God in the highest heaven, and on earth peace to those on whom his favor rests." When the angels had left them and gone into heaven, the shepherds said to one another, "Let's go to Bethlehem and see this thing that has happened, which the Lord has told us about."

"So they hurried off and found Mary and Joseph, and the baby, who was lying in the manger. When they had seen him, they spread the word concerning what had been told them about this child, and all who heard it were amazed at what the shepherds said to them."(NIV) Shaking her head at the wonderful memory, the tears started down her cheeks again.

"The shepherds never left Bethlehem that night. They laughed and said they left the angel Gabriel was watching the sheep! They went around the entire town knocking on doors at dawn, telling all Joseph's cousins that the Savior had been born, so we did end up in a nice house, and lots and lots of visitors." "We told them all that had happened, but they looked at Jesus as an ordinary baby and maybe with a little resentment for us."

CHAPTER EIGHTEEN

"O N THE EIGHTH DAY, WHEN it was time to circumcise the child, he was named Jesus, the name the angel had given him before he was conceived. When the time came for the purification rites required by the Law of Moses, Joseph and Mary took him to Jerusalem to present him to the Lord (as it is written in the Law of the Lord, "Every firstborn male is to be consecrated to the Lord"), and to offer a sacrifice in keeping with what is said in the Law of the Lord: "a pair of doves or two young pigeons."

"We stopped at the money changers that Jesus would come to despise and bought two doves. Walking up the steps of the temple we see coming right at us this very old man, looking as if he were walking as fast as he could. I looked at Joseph and he looked at me. I was glad Joseph had Jesus, because this kindly old man would have knocked me over if he had slipped and fell."

"Now there was a man in Jerusalem called Simeon, who was righteous and devout. He was waiting for the consolation of Israel, and the Holy Spirit was on him. It had been revealed to him by the Holy Spirit that he would not die before he had seen the Lord's Messiah. Moved by the Spirit, he went into the temple courts. When the parents brought in the child Jesus to do for him what the custom of the Law required, Simeon took him in his arms and praised God, saying: "Sovereign Lord, as you have promised, you may now dismiss your servant in peace. For my eyes have seen your salvation which you have prepared in the sight of all nations: a light for revelation to the Gentiles, and the glory of your people Israel."(NIV)

"Then Simeon blessed them and said to Mary, his mother: "This child is destined to cause the falling and rising of many in Israel, and to be a sign that will be spoken against, so that the thoughts of many hearts will be revealed. And a sword will pierce your own soul too."

"Joseph thanked him for his kind words and prophecy and we continued down the halls of the temple. Now we see an old woman, looking as if she is walking as fast as possible."

"There was also a prophet, Anna, the daughter of Penuel, of the tribe of Asher. Coming up to them at that very moment, she gave thanks to God and spoke about the child to all who were looking forward to the redemption of Jerusalem." (NIV)

Mary Magdalene looked at John and said," how do you deal with something like that?"

"Well, she must have kept it to herself all these years, because my father never said a word to me." John said.

"You are both right," Mother Mary said. "It was difficult not to say anything to my sister Salome or Joseph's brother Cleopas." The shepherds told them, but we didn't talk about it ever again. It certainly drew Joseph and me much closer, as it was the two of us that God had sent his messenger, Gabriel. God wanted people to discover Jesus the Savior of the World for themselves and let them choose to believe that He was the one who would save them from their sins and give them eternal life."

"We were not in a hurry to get back to Nazareth, so Joseph started woodworking projects for the people of Bethlehem. Things were going just fine, and then -the Magi turned up on their camels, fine robes and gifts and the neighborhood was in an uproar again."

"Magi from the east came to Jerusalem and asked, "Where is the one who has been born king of the Jews? We saw his star when it rose and have come to worship him. "When King Herod heard this he was disturbed, and all Jerusalem with him. When he had called together all the people's chief priests and teachers of the law, he asked them where the Messiah was to be born. "In Bethlehem in Judea," they replied, "for this is what the prophet has written: "'But you, Bethlehem, in the land of Judah, are by no means least among the rulers of Judah; for out of you will come a ruler who will shepherd my people Israel.' Then Herod called the Magi secretly and found out from them the exact time the star had appeared. He sent them to Bethlehem and said, "Go and search carefully for the child. As soon as you find him, report to me, so that I too may go and worship him."(NIV)

"After they had heard the king, they went on their way, and the star they had seen when it rose went ahead of them until it stopped over the place where the child was. When they saw the star, they were overjoyed. On coming to the house, they saw the child with his mother Mary, and they bowed down and worshiped him. Then they opened their treasures and presented him with gifts of gold, frankincense and myrrh. And having been warned in a dream not to go back to Herod, they returned to their country by another route." (NIV)

"Joseph had fallen asleep very early, and he had a vision from the angel Gabriel, who said, get up and get moving now, before King Herod kills the baby. We left town a little after midnight. Whatever we brought from Nazareth we took, whatever we needed for Jesus we took, loaded it on our donkey, Sarah and we were on our way to Egypt. We didn't tell anyone for their own safety where we were going."

"We heard later that Herod murdered every boy under the age of two in Bethlehem. We were so sad for our friends, and so thankful that once again the angel had been sent by God to keep Jesus safe. We decided from that time on, we would not tell anyone that Jesus was the Savior of the World. We knew God would announce it at the right time. So we lived in Egypt until King Herod died. When he died, our family had grown, we decided to move back to Nazareth and raise our family there, and continue not to say anything about Jesus."

"Jesus was a well behaved young man, helping Joseph in the shop, helping with the younger kids, but he gave us a scare when he was twelve. We decided we would take the family to the Passover since Jesus was twelve. We never had to worry about him, and we saw him with the other children talking to the teachers of the Law. He knew where we were staying and he knew when we were leaving. On our way home, we realize we don't have Jesus with us. At first we thought he was with the cousins, but the next day we find out he is not. So we left the rest of the children with Joseph's brother Cleopas and his wife Mary, and head back to Jerusalem to look for Jesus. I can't say we were worried, but we were the foster parents of the Savior of the Lord. We finally looked on the third day in the room with the teachers of the Law, only now there was an entire room of teachers now, and there is twelve year old Jesus asking questions. You just had to be there. It was just another amazing day in the life of Jesus. So we walked in, said hello to the teachers and said, 'Sorry, we have to take Jesus home now.' The teachers were just overwhelming in their praise of Jesus; said they never ever had another student like him."

"Heading out on the road and I say to my missing son, 'Why did you treat us like that? We have been looking for you for four days?"

"Jesus just looked me in the eye and said, 'Didn't you know I had to be in my Father's house?'(NIV)

"We kept walking and caught up with the family and he never caused me another moment of trouble, but it made me wonder if He knew that he was to be the Savior of the World."

"After that, He helped me with the younger children, helped Joseph in the shop, and when He was about to turn 30, our oldest daughter was getting married. We didn't order enough wine, and I went up to Jesus, and he looked at me and said, 'Woman, it is not my time.' I told the waiters, do whatever he says. Jesus told them to fill up all the water containers with water. I gave some to the groom's father, and he so surprised I saved the best wine until later."

"So after that He left the house. The first time I went to bring Him some food, I took the younger children with me, but they whined that they wanted to stay home with their friends. I started with my group of good friends visiting with food and clothes. We would just stop by where ever he was teaching, and bring food for him and his apostles. We did that for three years, and now, we won't be doing that anymore." More tears.

John was the next to speak. "The angel Gabriel told Zechariah, he would become a father and would not speak until John the Baptist was born. The angel Gabriel came to you and said you would become pregnant overshadowed by the Holy Spirit. Your fiancé Joseph had Gabriel appear to him and told him to go ahead and marry you. The angel Gabriel told the Magi and Joseph separately to leave and escape Herod and then the Angel Gabriel told you go come back to Nazareth."

It was ironic that John was so interested in the visions of angels, as he would spend his last days on earth writing about the visions of heaven that had been revealed to him in the Book of Revelation.

Mary said, "We lived a good life there, never knowing when Jesus would show that he was the Messiah.

I believe in God, I believe in Jesus. Even though I saw him die, I don't believe this is the end of the story. I will sit in my new chair that Jesus made me this week and sew."

Mary looked at him and said, "Why don't you nap? We are going at dawn to the grave site."

CHAPTER NINETEEN

JOHN SAID, "THE DISCIPLES PROBABLY will be at Mary's Upper Room."

Mary Magdalene said, "Ok. I might need to know that."

"When the Sabbath was over, Mary Magdalene, Mary the mother of James, and Salome bought spices so that they might go to anoint Jesus' body. Very early on the first day of the week, just after sunrise, they were on their way to the tomb and they asked each other, "Who will roll the stone away from the entrance of the tomb?"

"But when they looked up, they saw that the stone, which was very large, had been rolled away. As they entered the tomb, they saw a young man dressed in a white robe sitting on the right side, and they were alarmed."

"Don't be alarmed," he said. "You are looking for Jesus the Nazarene, who was crucified. He has risen! He is not here. See the place where they laid him. But go; tell his disciples and Peter, 'He is going ahead of you into Galilee. There you will see him, just as he told you. While they were wondering about this, suddenly two men in clothes that gleamed like lightning stood beside them. In their fright the women bowed down with their faces to the ground, but the men said to them, "Why do you look for the living among the dead? He is not here; he has risen! Remember how he told you, while he was still with you in Galilee: 'The Son of Man must be delivered over to the hands of sinners, be crucified and on the third day be raised again.' "Then they remembered his words." (NIV)

"When they came back from the tomb, they told all these things to the Eleven and to all the others. It was Mary Magdalene, Joanna, Mary the mother of James, and the others with them who told this to the apostles. But they did not believe the women, because their words seemed to them like nonsense. Peter, however, got up and ran to the tomb. Bending over, he saw the strips of linen lying by themselves, and he went away, wondering to himself what had happened." (NIV)

Mary Magdalene and Mother Mary were very persuasive. They insisted the disciples search their memories for the words that the Lord had spoken to them. Mother Mary put her arms out and pleaded, "Why can't you remember? Think! You know he is the Savior of the World. You know that rock is huge. Remember what Jesus said? if you have faith you can move mountains. Clear your heads and open your hearts."

Yet the disciples sat there befuddled at the turn of events. Yes, they knew both of the Marys would never tell an untruth, but emotionally, they could not open their hearts to hear.

The women left the Upper Room with unused spices in hand, not quite understanding, but believing that Jesus was alive, but they just didn't know where he was.

Not saying anything to the others, Mary Magdalene decided to go back and see if she could find Jesus. Peter said he would go back to the gravesite, especially if what the women had said was true, because it meant that Jesus wanted to see him. John wanted to go see for himself after listening to Mother Mary today and the day before.

"Peter and the other disciple started for the tomb. Both were running, but the other disciple outran Peter and reached the tomb first. He bent over and looked in at the strips of linen lying there but did not go in. Then Simon Peter came along behind him and went straight into the tomb. He saw the strips of linen lying there, as well as the cloth that had been wrapped around Jesus' head. The cloth was still lying in its place, separate from the linen. Finally the other disciple, who had reached the tomb, first, also went inside. He saw and believed. (They still did not understand from Scripture that Jesus had to rise from the dead.) Then the disciples went back to where they were staying."

"Now Mary stood outside the tomb crying. As she wept, she bent over to look into the tomb and saw two angels in white, seated where Jesus' body had been, one at the head and the other at the foot. They asked her, "Woman, why are you crying?"

"They have taken my Lord away," she said, "and I don't know where they have put him." At this, she turned around and saw Jesus standing there, but she did not realize that it was Jesus."

He asked her, "Woman, why are you crying? Who is it you are looking for?"

Thinking he was the gardener, she said, "Sir, if you have carried him away, tell me where you have put him, and I will get him."

Jesus said to her, "Mary." She turned toward him and cried out in Aramaic, "Rabboni!"

Jesus said, "Do not hold on to me, for I have not yet ascended to the Father. Go instead to my brothers and tell them, 'I am ascending to my Father and your Father, to my God and your God.'"

Mary Magdalene went to the disciples with the news: "I have seen the Lord!" And she told them that he had said these things to her."(NIV)

Now the disciples were all shaken. Mary Magdalene had seen the Lord and talked to the Lord. She told them Jesus had told her to go and talk to the disciples. Her joy was unmistakable. Any stranger off the street would find Mary Magdalene's story credible. They yawned, shook their heads, and tried so hard to accept what she was saying- but something kept the information from reaching their hearts.

Mary Magdalene left to find Mother Mary and the friends. As they were walking up and down the streets of Jerusalem, singing, praising God and stopping to tell everyone they saw that Jesus was alive. They stopped at the woodshop of James and Jude who gave hugs to each and every friend and their Mother. They had no problem believing that Jesus was alive. Mother Mary was like a young girl again, as she twirled and danced down the streets.

Back at the home of the high priest, Caiaphas didn't have any problem realizing that Jesus was alive. He paid off the guards and said, go home and don't say a word to anyone. He sat down and shook his head. Would that Jesus who plagued his life ever leave? Could he just please be able to be the high priest without the Messiah coming to earth when he finally got to be the high priest? Life was so unfair, and Caiaphas was very unhappy that Jesus again was alive.

The joy of Mother Mary and her friends was a living testimonial to the fact that Jesus had beaten death and the power of the devil and was indeed alive. Everyone in Jerusalem knew Mother Mary and her friends. They clapped and sang hymns of happiness as they saw the women dancing and singing down the streets of Jerusalem.

Jesus thought that the women would certainly be able to convince the disciples that He was alive. He saw that the women would not be enough to break the Lucifer curse put on the disciples on Thursday. He would need to make a couple of appearances and soon, so they could see He had indeed risen from the dead.

"After his suffering, he presented himself to them and gave many convincing proofs that he was alive. He appeared to them (twelve times) over a period of forty days and spoke about the kingdom of God." (NIV)

Afterward Jesus appeared again to his disciples, by the Sea of Galilee "I'm going out to fish," Simon Peter told them, and they said, "We'll go with you." So they went out and got into the boat, but that night they caught nothing.

Early in the morning, Jesus stood on the shore, but the disciples did not realize that it was Jesus. He called out to them, "Friends haven't you any fish? "No," they answered.

He said, "Throw your net on the right side of the boat and you will find some." When they did, they were unable to haul the net in because of the large number of fish. Then the disciple whom Jesus loved said to Peter, "It is the Lord!" As soon as Simon Peter heard him say, "It is the Lord," he wrapped his outer garment around him and jumped into the water."(NIV)

This was now a private time for Peter to spend with his Lord. What was said is unknown, but surely Peter asked for forgiveness and received it from His Lord. Certainly it was a time that Peter would always treasure in his heart.

"When they had finished eating, Jesus said to Simon Peter, "Simon son of John, do you love me more than these?"

"Yes, Lord," he said, "you know that I love you."

Jesus said, "Feed my lambs."

Again Jesus said, "Simon son of John, do you love me?"

He answered, "Yes, Lord, you know that I love you."

Jesus said, "Take care of my sheep."

The third time he said to him, "Simon son of John, do you love me?"

Peter was hurt because Jesus asked him the third time, "Do you love me?" He said, "Lord, you know all things; you know that I love you."

Jesus said, "Feed my sheep.

Very truly I tell you, when you were younger you dressed yourself and went where you wanted; but when you are old you will stretch out your hands, and someone else will dress you and lead you where you do not want to go." Jesus said this to indicate the kind of death by which Peter would glorify God. Then he said to him, "Follow me!" (NIV)

In this way Peter was able to repent of his denial of his Lord and Savior and know that his life would be to glorify God at all times.

Then the eleven disciples went to Galilee, to the mountain where Jesus had told them to go. When they saw him, they worshiped him; but some doubted. Then Jesus came to them and said, "All authority in heaven and on earth has been given to me. Therefore go and make disciples of all nations, baptizing them in the name of the Father and of the Son and of the Holy Spirit, and teaching them to obey everything I have commanded you. And surely I am with you always, to the very end of the age." (NIV)

If you love me, keep my commands. And I will ask the Father, and he will give you another advocate to help you and be with you forever—the Spirit of truth. The world cannot accept him, because it neither sees him nor knows him. But you know him, for he lives with you and will be in you. I will not leave you as orphans; I will come to you. Before long, the world will not see me anymore, but you will see me. Because I live, you also will live. On that day you will realize that I am in my Father, and you are in me, and I am in you. Whoever has my commands and keeps them is the one who loves me. The one who loves me will be loved by my Father, and I too will love them and show myself to them."

Then Judas (not Judas Iscariot) said, "But, Lord, why do you intend to show yourself to us and not to the world?"

Jesus replied, "Anyone who loves me will obey my teaching. My Father will love them, and we will come to them and make our home with them. Anyone who does not love me will not obey my teaching. These words you hear are not my own; they belong to the Father who sent me. (NIV)

"All this I have spoken while still with you. But the Advocate, the Holy Spirit, whom the Father will send in my name, will teach you all things and will remind you of everything I have said to you.

When he had led them out to the vicinity of Bethany, he lifted up his hands and blessed them. While he was blessing them, he left them and was taken up into heaven.

When he disappeared from sight, John remembered what he had told the disciples months before that he was leaving them.

"Peace I leave with you; my peace I give you. I do not give to you as the world gives. Do not let your hearts be troubled and do not be afraid. "(NIV).